Ten Principles of Black Self-Esteem

Letters of Heritage, Lessons of Hope

E. Hammond Oglesby

The Pilgrim Press
Cleveland, Ohio

DEDICATED TO MY GRANDFATHER,

JOHN ALEXANDER OGLESBY,

AND ALL THE ANCESTORS IN FAITH.

The Pilgrim Press, Cleveland, Ohio
© 1999 by E. Hammond Oglesby

DeLois C. Nance, "America," from *Urban Realities,* used by permission of
Swayzine Nance. • Enoch H. Oglesby, "I Believe," "Jesus Is My Big Brother,"
"Reachable Dreams," and "Did You Get the Point," from *Collaboration,* used by
permission of Rycraw Productions.

Biblical quotations are from the New Revised Standard Version of the Bible,
© 1989 by the Division of Christian Education of the National Council of the
Churches of Christ in the U.S.A., and are used by permission. Quotations
noted GNB are from the Good News Bible (New York: American Bible
Society, 1976).

04 03 02 01 00 99   5 4 3 2 1

Library of Congress Cataloging-in-Publication Data
Oglesby, Enoch H. (Enoch Hammond)
  Ten principles of black self-esteem : letters of heritage,
  lessons of hope / E. Hammond Oglesby.
    p. cm.
  ISBN 0-8298-1321-7 (pbk. : alk. paper)
  1. Self-esteem. 2. Self-esteem in children. 3. Self-esteem—
  Religious aspects—Christianity. 4. Afro-Americans—Psychology.
  I. Title.
 BF697.5.S46044 1999
 158.1'089'96073—dc21   98-50330
                     CIP

Ten Principles of Black Self-Esteem

1. Love God with your whole heart by first demonstrating the ethno-relative power of love for black people; let black-on-black love replace black-on-black violence.

2. Honor and respect your elders and ancestors, who faced and conquered the world's persecution and who found the presence of peace within.

3. Do not trust another individual to do for you what you alone can do for yourself; trust only in God.

4. Remember always that black history did not begin with slavery, but with ancient Egyptian kings, queens, scientists, sages, and artisans of mother Africa.

5. Do not forget your forebears who once were slaves; who endured the trauma of the Middle Passage; who landed in Jamestown, Virginia, in 1619; and who gallantly fought—by God's grace—to win the prize of freedom from their white oppressors.

6. Choose peace over confusion, righteousness over unrighteousness, and life over death as you walk among the people.

7. Remember that self-love is not the denial of the value of black personhood.

8. Listen first with a heart of love without first judging with a heart of stone another's action.

9. Throw down ropes from the mountain of success rather than scissors, so each person—black or white—might climb.

10. Remember always that ordinary ability among humans becomes extraordinary under the protective wings of God.

Contents

Preface

Ten Principles of Black Self-Esteem explores principles that can be used to build self-esteem among black people in America. Throughout life people will degrade you and put you down simply because of physical appearance, size, social status, or the color of your skin. But when God made us, God made us to be the flowers of human creation, not weeds in the garden to be trampled upon. There is so much negative energy in our culture today, which denies our right to grow; and therefore, it tends to pull the human spirit to the ground. Yet we are challenged by an old African proverb to remember the following: "If you make yourself a doormat, people will wipe their feet on you."

This book includes two forms of writing: personal letters and descriptive chapters. The letters represent a poetic meditation on the frailties and hopes of black family life in America and the promise of God's unconditional love and grace. I hope that this book will encourage groups and families to discuss the critical issues examined in the letters.

The other chapters provide a foundational understanding of the dynamic and emergent principles of black self-esteem. Many streams of thought are possible in the search for authentic personhood or self-esteem. Conceptually, part of my task has been to name the sources and streams of self-esteem from the diverse religious and moral traditions in American culture. For example, the chapters "Lifting Up an Afrocentric Biblical Legacy" and "Recovering Hope from Martin and Malcolm" are attempts to better understand some of the biblical and historical themes and values articulated in the events leading up to and including the Million Man March.

A principle may be defined as a foundational truth or an ultimate norm upon which other things are based. Derived from the Latin word *principium,* which means basis or origin, *principle* can also be defined as an ultimate basis or cause, or an adherence to a rule of conduct as a center of the moral life. Some examples of what I shall call principles in this book include love, faith, freedom, integrity, esteem or self-regard, and respect for the elders in the human community.

The distinguishing feature of the term *principle,* in contrast to *command,* is that it indicates the quality (such as love) that should be present in every moral act or relationship: from parent to child, from father to son, from father to daughter, from brotha to brotha, from brotha to sister, and ultimately from humans to God. In short, I will analyze the sociohistorical and religious context out of which the ten dominant principles of self-esteem seem to emerge for blacks in America.

Some crucial questions that claim our attention for discussion include the following: What is self-esteem for a people whose backs have been pressed against the walls of adversity and oppression (see the chapter "Ten Principles of Black Self-Esteem")? What is the relationship between the Million Man March and the Promise Keepers (see "Making Small and Large Differences")? What is the use of or authority of the Bible for the moral life (see "Lifting Up an Afrocentric Biblical Legacy")? What does it mean to recover hope in child–parent relationships (see "Recovering Hope from Martin and Malcolm")? What does the Bible say about angels and so-called guardian angels (see "Being Touched by Angels")? These are just some of the critical questions and issues we shall struggle with in this volume.

Open Letter to the Man on the Mall

JUDGE NOT THE BROTHER! THERE ARE SECRETS IN HIS HEART THAT
YOU MIGHT WEEP TO SEE.

—Egbert Martin

The very time I thought I was lost,
My dungeon shook
And my chains fell off.

—African American Folk Saying

Dear Nameless Man on the Mall,

It was 7:02 A.M. when I arrived at the Washington Mall on that crisp autumn day of October 16, 1995. The majestic power of the sun had already arisen from the eastern horizon and gently kissed the earth's trees and bushes and turned them into an autumn gold, as the imposing statue of Abraham Lincoln, the reluctant emancipator, looked on in amazing silence at the sons and daughters of mother Africa.

History has always been partial to irony and surprise. And I think that one of the profound ironies of black presence in America is the bewitching irony that the sons and daughters of Africa are *still* struggling to be free and equal—right down to the present moment! I spotted this in you, but I am getting ahead of my story.

Do you recall the moment? The full crowd on that special day had not yet arrived at the graceful dawning of the morning. No speeches had been made. No massive D.C. security force had visually appeared. No public dignitaries, politicians, or preachers that I could readily recognize had yet arrived. Perhaps some were there among the pockets of people scattered along the vast landscape of the Washington Mall.

Now as I walked among the pockets of people, the language of silence and expectation flooded my consciousness as I wondered what the full day would bring. Moving through pockets of the early gathering, suddenly I overheard—from a distance—your voice as you said to another, "Brotha-man, I'm glad to be here . . . but what is atonement?"

Months later, your question still lingered in my head and heart as I taught ethics and theology at Eden Theological Seminary. I began writing this book as an attempt to think through the answers to your question and to unpack the curiously simple, yet profoundly complex gifts of faith, reason, and conscience.

You may ask, which one of the three gifts do I follow? Certainly, the gift of faith is essential. Indeed, Holy Scriptures teach us that "faith is the assurance of things hoped for, the conviction of things not seen" (Hebrews 11:1). But with the other two gifts, I tend to trust conscience more than reason, because reason can be used as a tool of evil, racism, and greed. Thus I am more likely to agree with the French philosopher Jean-Jacques Rousseau, who said, "Reason deceives—conscience never."

The answer to the fundamental theological question "What is atonement?" has sociological and biblical implications for people of color and for all of humanity. In a multiracial and multicultural society, the question of atonement is ethically tied to the biblical imperative to "love one another" in good times and bad times and to practice the "power of forgiveness," beginning with our beautiful black selves as children of God. Perhaps by so doing, we may grasp a deeper understanding of God's liberating grace and sacrificial love among black people as well as for others in human community. Concerning the communal power of sacrificial love, Holy Scriptures affirm, "No one has greater love than this, to lay down one's life for one's friends" (John 15:13).

Definition and Declaration

Mall man, this letter may seem preachy, but that is only because I did not take the opportunity to meet you and talk with you that morning. Yet, I must speak because your voice and concerns remain on my mind and heart.

In the life and faith of the religious person, the word *atonement* is a theological term that means "an individual's oneness with God" and points to a process of bringing those who are alienated, estranged, and disenfranchised into unity with God.

Is this not what we were seeking from the Million Man March? Is this not its plain truth? But we cannot break open our future with hope; we cannot embrace the burdens of history as our heritage until we press further. I do not know your heritage, so let me speak from the passions of my own.

The word *atonement* occurs in the Old Testament to translate words from the KPR word group, and it is found once in the New Testament materials, rendering *katallagé* (which is better translated *reconciliation*).[1] The literal translation of the term *KPR* means to "cover over or wash away."[2] In the context of religious experience, the term refers to the washing away or the obliteration of one's sins. In Christian theology, for instance, atonement denotes the mighty works of Jesus Christ in dealing with the problem of sin in human creation and in bringing sinners into right relation with the very ground and source of our being, namely, God.[3]

In view of how our people have suffered, I sometimes bristle at the Holy Scripture's underlying claim. All have sinned and come short of the glory of God, the Merciful and Loving One (Romans 3:2–13, Jeremiah 14:20, 40:3, Luke 15:18, Ephesians 4:26). Scripture reminds us of the need for atonement in the moral life, simply because all unrighteousness is sin.

Now dear brother, we need atonement because it is a precondition of empowerment. The need does not stop with African Americans living in the United States. The need for atonement is part and parcel of the universal human predicament. Human beings are caught in the predicament of sin from the White House to the outhouse, from the country shacks of old plantations that dotted the landscape of Jim Crowism in Mississippi during the 1890s to the streets of Beacon Hill near the Boston Commons in Massachusetts in the 1990s. The reality of sin is present both in the world and in us.

Therefore, the need for atonement can be seen as a confessional dress rehearsal for empowerment and is essentially brought about by three things:

- First, the universality of sin and our lack of courage as sometimes deceptive individuals and hypocrites (for example, "there is none that doeth good, no, not one" [Psalm 14:3])
- Second, the seriousness of sin in the world; concretely, the sin of racism is ever before the church and the nation as a form of original sin, and
- Third, man's or woman's inability to deal with the gravity of sin.[4]

Fundamentally, what I am confessing to you, Mall Man, is simply that all of these conditions relative to the human predicament of sin (either the sin of racism or what Augustine called sin as pride) pointed this massive wave of sojourners in the direction of the Washington Mall on Monday, October 16, 1995.

What, then, did we declare as worthy of remembrance, in terms of the impact of this day upon the consciousness of black men? Here is the voice of Robert C. Adams, another proud brother, from jail:

> The Black men here at Carson City Correctional Facility sat in awe of the sea of Black men . . . each here trying to constrain the tears in our eyes and each attentively gripping his own piece of joy, pain and hope. Who else has more to atone for than the Black man in prison? . . . That night, for the first time in six years, I wrote my ex-wife and children and asked for their forgiveness.[5]

Three Fruits of Atonement

The need for forgiveness that Robert Adams felt also touched me. Did it also tap you on the shoulder, Mall Man? Adams points out that the first fruit of atonement is, namely, a willingness to do the right thing, to make a change in one's life.

The moral life is all about making difficult choices in life. Those who decided to participate in the Million Man March made a deliberate moral choice. Those who chose to stay away also made a deliberate choice. Many wives, lovers, and well-wishers who decided to spiritually and symbolically support the brothers who journeyed to Washington, D.C., by staying home from work, holding gender-based discussion groups and prayer vigils, or wearing the liberation colors of red, black, and green on the streets of America made a deliberate moral choice. To be an "atoner" means to be a moral agent. It means that the atoner is one who deliberately engages in the moral struggle to do the right thing.

You and I were there. But even more, I suspect that as a moral agent, the atoner seeks an understanding and critical assessment of the life-and-death issues that confront poor and marginalized people in contemporary society. Your question was a start in this direction. The real substance of atonement is not a set of rituals that pious people follow, but rather an invitation to communal dialogue and renewal as the human self struggles to find its own center of meaning and purpose.

The atoner seeks this critical understanding of life's choices, and then proceeds on the basis of conscience to will that which is good and right for the amelioration of the black condition in America. For example, the critically acclaimed film producer and director Spike Lee strongly suggested to us, in the movie *Get On the Bus,* that the ethical imperative "Do the right thing" is not a simple possibility. At best, it is an agonizing dilemma of the head and heart.

It requires every morally honest person to reflect upon these questions: What does it mean to be a whole self—mind, soul, will, feeling—in light of the perennial problem of white racism in America? How can I do the right thing in a nation so deeply divided by race and religion? Why do we seem to only be concerned about what's right and wrong, until our rights have been wronged?

It has been said and some believe that only truth will set us free. But I am compelled to raise another question: *Whose truth* will set us free? Truth requires both the risk of faith and the risk of self-discovery. For example, without risk there is neither self-discovery (a sense of esteem) nor faith (a sense of trust)—only despair and estrangement of blacks and whites in American communities. Historically, I am reminded of the keen observations of Alexis de Tocqueville, the distinguished French scholar who noted quite early in the formation of our nation the paradox and future dilemma of the black presence: "The most formidable of all the ills that threaten the future of the Union arises from the presence of a black population upon its territory. The whites and the blacks are placed in the situation of two foreign communities. These two races are fastened to each other without intermingling; and they are unable to separate entirely or to combine."[6]

A second fruit of atonement as imagined through the experience of the Million Man March is the courage to be black—in spite of the painful lessons of American history. I mean to suggest that some of us who navigate the mainstream of American life seem to be overly sensitive to what I call the "Integrationist Syndrome." By this, Mall Man, I mean when a black man becomes economically successful or famous in the dominant culture, he has a tendency to play down the African part of his identity and ethnic heritage in favor of a more acceptable European or Asian part of his cultural and family heritage.

Is this a matter of selective self-acceptance of one's heritage? I wish that we could have discussed this. It seems to me that even raising these questions about ethnic traits and family heritage shows signs of a racist society, of promoting or valuing white culture over black culture.

As moral agents, if we feel compelled to choose—and we do— why not equally choose the positive traits and virtues from both parts of one's heritage? Can cultural diversity give us a composite, integrative view of human selfhood? Analytically, I suspect that the fruit of atonement in relation to blackness here means that the atoner must stop looking at cultural heritage vertically (in the form of hierarchies by which one has to be better than another). Rather one must attempt to see it horizontally, that is to say, as a tapestry, which weaves together all of the colorful fibers and fragments of one's own identity and rich psychosocial and religio-spiritual heritage. Perhaps herein lies the source of true empowerment.

Furthermore, as a theologian, father, and proud black man, I want to claim all that I am. And what I claim is this: I am a black man of African descent living in America. Pure and simple, that was good enough for my father, Joe Nathan Oglesby, and it is good enough for me. But such a fact of my personal existence in America is neither pure nor simple. Existentially, to be a black man in white America is never a simple fact or easy existence. Therefore, to live in the skin or walk in the shoes of a black man is a difficult and complex spiritual pilgrimage.

To be sure, one is in need of atonement and grace on a daily basis, and not just through the fanfare of a symbolic march on the Washington Mall. As moral agent the atoner is compelled to grapple with these ethical questions: After the March, then what am I to do? Who am I to be? What have I brought back from the March that can benefit the community? Who am I to be as a result of one's pilgrimage to what some brothers on the ghetto streets call the "Chocolate City"? These types of questions and concerns cannot be easily ignored either by the organizers of the Million Man March or the average American citizen, who may hold Tiger Woods in high esteem for his professional achievements and abilities. Of course, I am one of those citizens who feel proud of his personal achievements and history-making feats in the world of golf! But as an atoner, I deeply lament his apparent ambivalence about blackness—while at the same time affirming one's claim as a moral agent to the right most basic to us as human beings, namely, the right of self-definition.

I believe that the real fruit of atonement, implicitly or explicitly expressed by the participants of the Million Man March, is the invitation to recover and embrace a certain cultural and spiritual particularity. In his critically acclaimed book *There Is a River,* Vincent Harding has suggested that black people are essentially a spiritual people, in terms of one's understanding, histori-cally, of the meaning of black struggle for freedom in America.[7]

For Harding, present suffering experienced by blacks can be understood only because African Americans have developed cer-tain spiritual resources to deal with the demonic forces, racial injustices, and moral contradictions of history. As an atoner, I believe that the gift of spiritual particularity energizes a battered and tired people to continue to struggle for justice, equity, and meaning. In short, the reality of spiritual particularity for the atoner is a way of engaging the marginalized groups in society in the search for meaning.

The quest for meaning in history is a by-product of the jour-ney toward atonement. Here Harding echoes the historical signif-icance of the quest for meaning:

> A sense of meaning—which we surely create out of our par-ticular responses to the "facts" of experience—is crucial if we are to join ourselves to the past and the future, to com-mune with the ancestors as well as the coming children. Without it we lose touch with ourselves, our fellow humans, and other creatures, with the earth our mother, and with the cosmos itself. Without the search for meaning, the quest for vision, there can be no authentic movement toward libera-tion, no true identity or radical integration for an individ-ual or a people.[8]

A Black Army of Community Volunteers

The ethics of voluntarism is as old as America itself. According to *Merriam Webster's Collegiate Dictionary,* the popular concept of voluntarism so pervasive in contemporary American culture actu-ally encompasses four key notions:

Derivative of the Latin word *voluntarius,* the concept refers to "one who enters into, or offers his or herself, for service of one's own free will"

The notion refers to the "moral principle of supporting anything by reliance upon voluntary action" on the part of people in the community

"One who enters into service voluntarily as opposed to conscript"

"A piece of work" rooted in the principle of self-help

Combined together, the dynamic notion of voluntarism includes acting, discerning, and deciding on the basis of one's own values, moral conscience, and self-esteem.

The ethical imperatives before the black community on the second anniversary of the Million Man March is economic empowerment and spiritual revitalization. Both of these views are deeply rooted in the philosophy of "self-help" as reflected by the black prophetic leaders throughout history—from the American revolutionary Chrispus Attucks to General Colin Powell. The leaders include such heavyweights as Mary McLeod Bethune, Harriet Tubman, Frederick Douglass, David Walker, Marcus Garvey, and Booker T. Washington—just to name a few. For example, Booker T. Washington's moral view of the economically self-sufficient black person was the view that a hardworking laborer can have his own business. He observed, "Every member of the race who succeeds in business, however humble and simple that business may be, because he has learned the important lessons of cleanliness, promptness, system, honesty, and progressiveness, is contributing his share in smoothing the pathway for this and succeeding generations."[9] Here Booker T. Washington's philosophy of voluntarism seems to be rooted in the Macedonian cry, "Cast down your buckets where you are!" To be sure, the ethical imperative today is a call for the formation of a black army of community volunteers. The idea is that each person must "give something back" to the wider community.

For example, in spring 1997 retired general Colin Powell emerged as the moral leader of a new army of volunteers dedicated to the proposition that all Americans have something to contribute— whether your ethnic hat is red, yellow, black, brown, or white— in rebuilding and revitalizing economically deprived neighborhoods throughout the United States. Colin Powell challenges the troops both in corporate America and in the trenches of inner-city neighborhoods to join the campaign of those who want to feed the poor, clothe the homeless, uplift the downtrodden, and mentor the young.

As a man of faith, I think the ethics of atonement can lead to empowerment. This can, in turn, lead directly to community involvement, spiritual development, economic employment, and mentoring programs in every church, mosque, and synagogue in our fragile global village where poor and destitute people cry to us and to God for compassion and for relief from suffering. In short, the ethics of atonement through the instrument of voluntarism shouts three things: "Feed my people!"; "Care for those who have been neglected and for those who have suffered in your own local communities through private and government programs and education enrichment and urban revitalization"; and "Each individual with God is a majority." "You can make a difference, I can make a difference in some child's life" is the dominant echo that came from the Presidential Volunteer Summit held in Philadelphia, Pennsylvania, in the spring of 1997.[10] Well, where are we today? Where do we go from here? What have we really achieved after bringing together over 2,000 community participants and elected officials from 140 communities?

Looking back to the Million Man March and the President's Volunteer Summit, I am reminded of the prophetic and politically relevant comment by the late Supreme Court Justice Thurgood Marshall concerning black progress in our democratic republic: "The question is not how far have we come, but how close are we . . . in reaching the promised land of freedom, justice, equality, for all." The ethics of atonement challenge us to reach out beyond the middle-class comfort zones of materialism, self-aggrandizement, competition, and social posturing to help others in need of God's liberating grace.

In summary, the ethics of atonement point the morally honest person in the direction of empowerment, reconciliation, and restoration of that which is broken—spiritually, culturally, economically, and materially—and must be fixed in our shattered lives. Atonement is not for false prophets, preachers, or politicians but for ordinary people of faith who march to the beat of a different drum, who can still catch the vision in the wilderness of white America, and who can still hear the quiet inner voice beyond the noise and tumult of the mass crowd that gathered at the Washington Mall on that unforgettable autumn day, Monday, October 16, 1995. Ordinary people of faith know that atonement is not a performance, but a profession, not a crafted speech given on a well-lighted stage, but a divine initiative of the human heart.

Finally, my unmet friend, ordinary people of faith know that true atonement begins as we welcome the "stranger" inside ourselves. Therefore, ordinary people of faith dare not forget that faith itself is a triadic mirror through which we see the face of God, the face of the family, and the face of the "stranger" crying out for help and affirmation. Holy Scriptures affirm: "For I was hungry and you gave me food, I was thirsty and you gave me something to drink, I was a stranger and you welcomed me, I was naked and you gave me clothing, I was sick and you took care of me, I was in prison and you visited me" (Matthew 25:35–37).

Ten Principles of Black Self-Esteem

"Teacher, which commandment in the law is the greatest?"
He said to him, "You shall love the Lord your God
with all your heart, with all your soul, with all your
mind. . . . And a second is like it: You shall love your
neighbor as yourself."

—Matthew 22:36–39

I was an intellectually curious yet reluctant participant in the Million Man March. The word *commandment* does not fall easily from my lips. It must be something about human nature because most people I know do not take easily to the notion of being under another individual's control. From a psycho-historical perspective, there is something, seemingly, in the body politic of the African personality construct that strongly resists and rebels against any form of direct authority. Perhaps this impulse toward rebellion against command language or authority is universal. Deep in my soul, I feel ambivalent because command language conjures up the images and painful scars of chattel slavery that African people had to endure for more than 375 years under white racism in America.

Notwithstanding, we are still stuck psychologically with a covenantal marriage between a people and their God—bound by a book known as the Bible, the people's living story of faith and deliverance, that commands authority over all creation. How majestic is its authority over human creation; how splendid is its storytelling power; and how profound is its wisdom and love to invest and risk so much in the sinful frame of humankind, by sending Jesus, the Child of God, to die on the cross. He rose on the third day, according to Scripture, as an *atonement* for the sins of the whole world! Musing upon the profound mystery and love of God, there is once again that marvelous word *atonement*, which was the spiritual centerpiece of the Million Man March a few years ago.

Meanwhile, the scope of our discussion here is, in part, around the word *commandments*, in relation to principles. Living always at the intersection of hope and despair, the morally honest person must raise some basic questions: What is a commandment? For people of color who are daily victimized by racial bigotry in America, what does it mean to use *command* language? What is a command? In modern society, we have observed that people often resist or pay little attention to commands—except in cases of their own self-interest. Etymologically speaking, the word *command* is derived from the Latin word *com-mandare*, which translates "to commit to," "to order." So then, the biblical idea of commandment means that the believer is one who acts under the power of the Commander: Almighty God.

Conceptually, we must emphasize in our proposed discussion of self-esteem that principles can also function as directional norms in child–parent relationships, especially among people with a shared memory of suffering and hope. For example, the Million Man March on one level was all about the fundamental moral struggle and agony of people of color to find directional norms for twenty-first century America. We may also point out that rules differ from principles or commandments in that they are concrete standards for particular types of situations.[1]

Too often in America people of color are faced daily with racism in spite of the nation's credo of liberty, justice, equality. Thus, we need commands as well as moral commanders at the highest levels of the government and the church to demand relief from racism. This bold imperative on the part of the believer would undoubtedly require nothing less than cultural and spiritual transformation. It would require nothing less than a change in the habits of each and every U.S. citizen. Ultimately, what is at stake is our relationship to God, the Holy One and Giver of Life.

This notion of the command means that the believer must be in obedience and submission to the Holy One who gives comfort and life. The believer or moral agent is, therefore, literally obligated to commit to the will of the Divine Commander. Hence, there is a binding claim upon all the participants and supporters of the Million Man March to commit to one another, not on the basis of politics, ideology, or denominational doctrine, but in the spirit of unconditional love. That is the point and logic of unconditional love—inclusive of the needs, hurts, and hopes of black people and of all people.

The command to love is both vertical and horizontal in human community. Ethically, the command to love has the power to transcend the troublesome religious divisions, ideologies, and isms that boldly parade the cultural landscape of America. I believe that the command to love engenders a spiritual capacity in us all that can transcend the walls of biblical or Islamic fundamentalism. I believe that the Million Man March was largely about accepting diversity, while affirming particularity within the religio-cultural heritage of the African American experience.

Brothers and sisters, if we learned anything about ourselves from this historical march it is that love is key. Love is respect for our sisters; love is respect for our brothers; love is respect for our daughters and sons; and love is respect for our spouses or significant others. Love is respect and reverence for the elders and foreparents, the warriors and sages that had the courage and strength of steel to light a candle in the wilderness of white America rather than to curse the long night of chattel slavery. Love is reverence to God, who called a people—the most wretched and despised of North America—from the status of nobodies to make them somebodies.

For example, the traditional black preacher of the old South would often remind churchgoers on Sunday morning that "there is no secret what God can do" and would lead them in singing "God got the whole world in his hand." Indeed, these powerful gospel lyrics serve notice to an oppressive system that God can take a despised people and make them into a royal people:

> But you are a chosen race, a royal priesthood, a holy nation, God's own people, in order that you may proclaim the mighty acts of him who called you out of darkness into his marvelous light. Once you were not a people, but now you are God's people; once you had not received mercy, but now you have received mercy. (1 Peter 2:9–10)

Hence, the integrative key of the Million Man March is still one of love for one another (our beautiful black selves), the neighbor, and God. Accordingly, the Bible teaches:

> When the Pharisees heard that he had silenced the Sadducees, they gathered together, and one of them, a lawyer, asked him a question to test him. "Teacher, which commandment in the law is the greatest?" He said to him, " 'You shall love the Lord your God with all your heart, and with all your soul, and with all your mind.' This is the greatest and first commandment. And a second is like it: 'You shall love your neighbor as yourself.' On these two commandments hang all the law and the prophets." (Matthew 22:34–40)

The ten principles of black self-esteem begin with taking responsibility for one's own actions and behavior. Ethically, the centerpiece of these evolving principles is love. Love is active. Love is goodwill. Love is justice distributed in behalf of the poor and hurting ones. Love is the power to overcome adversity and racial degradation in the world. Love is forgiving without forgetfulness. Love is giving back as a sign of gratitude for protection and nurture in a dangerous world, where white men can still lynch black men without wearing hoods and white sheets, but wearing pinstripes and double-breasted suits on Wall Street! Amidst the burden of being black in America, love takes on the clamor of moral struggle to literally achieve higher ground in the sociocultural system.

Looking back, I remember Maya Angelou, one of the key womanist voices at the Million Man March, who shared a poetic display of courage and wisdom. As I listened to her and countless other speakers, I mused silently on the meaning of black love, in light of an excerpt describing Maya's eighth-grade graduation ceremony in Stamps, Arkansas, in 1940. She recalls customary gift giving as a sign of love:

> Among Negroes the tradition was to give presents to children going only from one grade to another. How much more important this was when the person was graduating at the top of the class. Uncle Willie and Momma had sent away for a Mickey Mouse watch like Bailey's. Louise gave me four embroidered handkerchiefs. (I gave her three crocheted doilies.) Mrs. Sneed, the minister's wife, made me an underskirt to wear for graduation, and nearly every customer gave me a nickel or maybe even a dime with the instruction "Keep on moving to higher ground," or some such encouragement.[2]

Now when you educate a young man on the power of love in the struggle for racial justice and reconciliation, the spirit of the Million Man March would have us never forget the prophetic words and wisdom of Martin Luther King Jr., who wrote:

> I am convinced that love is the most durable power in the world. It is not an expression of impractical idealism, but of practical realism. Far from being the pious injunction of a Utopian dreamer, love is an absolute necessity for the survival of our civilization. To return hate for hate does nothing but intensify the existence of evil in the universe. Someone must have sense enough and religion enough to cut off the chain of hate and evil, and this can only be done through love. Moreover, love is creative and redemptive. Love builds up and unites; hate tears down and destroys. The aftermath of the "fight fire with fire" method . . . is bitterness and chaos; the aftermath of the love method is reconciliation and the creation of the beloved community. . . . Yes, love—which means understanding, creative, redemptive goodwill, even for one's enemies—is the solution to the race problem.[3]

The actor Ossie Davis once said, "One labors for what one loves, and one loves for what one labors." In a deep communal sense; love is the spiritual glue that holds together the ten principles of black self-esteem. Like the garment of good manners, love begins at home and must be worn abroad. The keepers and vanguards of black culture and moral tradition would remind us that there is no difficulty that love cannot conquer in human life.

There is no mountain that love cannot climb. There is no gulf that agape love cannot bridge between brotha and brotha, between brotha and sister, between father and son, between father and daughter, and ultimately between brotha and God. This is the primary moral lesson that has been instilled in black people, the nation, and the world. The ten principles of black self-esteem may serve as moral directives for all of us who take seriously the importance of a Christian perspective on self-esteem. Let us now take a closer look:

1. Love God with your whole heart by first demonstrating the ethno-relative power of love for black people; let black-on-black love replace black-on-black violence (Exodus 20:13, Galatians 6:2).

American churches and social institutions have never been able to undo the mess created by racism and the lingering pain of Jim Crowism heaped upon the shoulders of blacks, children and adults alike. Historically, the bold establishment in our society of separate but equal facilities for blacks and whites—which found legal sanction with the Supreme Court ruling in the *Plessy v. Ferguson* case of 1896—set into motion a customary pattern of low self-esteem that many black people still find hard to eliminate, psychologically and culturally, a century later. The problem is not simply theological—that is to say, the question of the moral capacity to love "the Lord God with one's whole heart"—but it is also psychosocial, in the sense of the perceived need to move from black-on-black violence or aggression to the posture of black-on-black love or genuine self-respect.

Therefore, the first functional principle of self-esteem between children and parents, between fathers and their sons, between mothers and their daughters is the principle of ethno-relative love. The basic notion behind such a principle is implied in the old adage that charity begins at home and spreads abroad. Hence, the ethically sensitive person is inclined to affirm that the real power of love cannot be found, necessarily, in philosophical systems of Platonic reasoning or Cartesian dualism.

The real power of love arises from the need of one human being to relate to another. Such a love is both active and relational. It cannot be coerced or intimidated by the threats of violence and punishment. From the perspective of the black experience, we may call this particular life force the ethno-relative power of love to transform the destructive pattern of black-on-black violence to constructive patterns of black-on-black love. This must be a moral precondition along the journey toward full self-esteem.

For troubled youths and young adults alike, I suspect that to embrace the concept of the ethno-relative power of love for black people means to let go of gang banging, rage, and abuse. It means to literally allow oneself to be fully human through the transforming power of love, to do a new thing in the life of the ordinary person. It means to let black-on-black love replace black-on-black violence. I believe that genuine self-esteem is, ultimately, rooted in our recognition that we are loved by God. As communities of moral struggle and promise, it is good to know that we are, indeed, loved by God. The first source of love, as the grounding of our being and self-worth, is God. Holy Scriptures affirm the universal principles of mutual love for one another as brothers and sisters in Christ:

> We love because he first loved us. Those who say, I love God, and hate their brothers and sisters, are liars; for those who do not love a brother or sister whom they have seen, cannot love God whom they have not seen. The commandment we have from him is this: those who love God must love their brothers and sisters also. (1 John 4:19–21)

2. Honor and respect your elders and ancestors, who faced and conquered the world's persecution and who found the presence of peace within (Exodus 3:16–18, Ruth 4:11–12, Psalm 107:32, John 16:33).

The first African American novelist, William Wells Brown, once remarked, "We are what we remember!" This is a very profound insight into the human condition because it implies that the progress, innovations, moral strides, and cultural achievements of the contemporary person have their origins in the past. As a pilgrim people of faith and struggle, we stand today upon the broad shoulders of our elders and ancestors.

Our ancestors confronted and endured the Middle Passage, the brutal pain of colonialism and mob violence. Our ancestors confronted and endured the rape and sexual abuse of our women and children. Our ancestors gave hope—historically speaking—to a destitute people to press against the dehumanizing system of chattel slavery because we serve a God of justice who is not finished with us.

In quiet moments of reflection upon the value of self-esteem—at those points in the human spirit where the painful lessons of history become living testimonies to God's grace and love—I am often reminded of the wisdom of Martin Luther King Jr. on the question of black progress:

> "We ain't all we ought to be; we ain't all we gonna be, but thank God, we're better than what we were!" I don't know for sure, but I suspect that Martin Luther King, Jr., for example, would undoubtedly echo the theological sentiment of the French poet Henri Ameil on the value of self-esteem being, partially, rooted in moral struggle—especially for a people with a common memory of suffering and hope.
>
> > Do not despise your present situation; for in it you must act, suffer, and conquer—knowing that from every point in the universal, you are equally near to heaven and the Infinite.[4]

Tiny sparkles of self-esteem are like gold nuggets from the rich mines of African soil. They sparkle and tingle because their source emanates from the spirit of the elders and ancestors and from the presence of the Infinite. What I am trying to suggest is that in the religion and culture of African people, the individual who seeks to live right is never outside the protection and spiritual presence of the ancestors. The spirit of the ancestors seems to function as a moral guide or ontological balance between God and humanity in present situations of danger.

So we honor our elders and ancestors. The principle of self-esteem is really tied into a mind-set and moral fabric rooted in the religion and culture of African people. For this reason, John S. Mbiti, in *African Religions and Philosophies,* speaks eloquently about the ontological link between God, the ancestral spirits, and humanity. He declares:

> An ontological balance must be maintained between God and man, the spirits and man, the departed and the living. When this balance is upset, people experience misfortunes and sufferings, or fear that these will strike them. The making of sacrifices . . . is also a psychological device to restore this ontological balance. It is also an act and occasion of making and renewing contact between God and man, the spirits and man, i.e. the spiritual and the physical worlds.[5]

In traditional African religion and culture, one may conclude that certain tokens of respect for the elders and ancestors can, in fact, undergird the bonds of self-esteem by providing children and adults with a moral link to the struggles and aspirations of past generations. Thus each person's life must be defined and informed by one's respect for, and nurturing of, the illuminating presence of the ancestors as a guide in the formation of human community.

To be sure, the conscious and direct exposure of this illuminating presence can not only enhance self-esteem in the heart and mind of the individual believer, but can also arouse a greater loyalty to the wholeness of God's peace within. In short, what we celebrate as a gift of self-esteem is nothing less than what Professor Mbiti calls the process of restoring ontological balance to our fragmented lives in a troubled world. Speaking plainly, to honor one's elders and ancestors empowers us all to restore the balance and to find peace to live a victorious life.

Indeed, Jesus himself cautioned his disciples, while giving them a word of hope in a world full of trouble. He said, "I have said this to you, so that in me you may have peace. In the world you face persecution. But take courage; I have conquered the world" (John 16:33).

3. "Thou shalt not trust another individual to do for you what you alone can do for yourself; trust only in God" (Galatians 6:5, Matthew 11:30, Psalm 146:3–4).

A third principle of self-esteem that both children and parents must come to terms with is the principle of self-reliance in the community. For people of color the impulse to dream of or to achieve a better life through higher learning is not something that white society can put inside us. A child who is to be successful in life must not only be reared in a loving and nurturing environment, but he or she must know the hard lessons of growing up black or poor in America. For example, no greater injury can be done to any youth than to deny him or her a sense of self-reliance and the confidence to trust in self rather than another.

No matter how degraded blacks, Latinos, Asians, Native Americans, and other people of color may ultimately feel by the demon of white racism, there still remains the moral question of responsibility. If history has taught us anything, then it is the difficult lesson of moral struggle and the acceptance of responsibility for our own dreams and nightmares, our own fortunes and failures. As the abolitionist Frederick Douglass said so eloquently over a century ago, "If there is no struggle, there is no progress."

Moral struggle for that which is right and good is a core value undergirding the principle of self-reliance. As people of faith and conscience, why ask another people to do for us what we alone must do for ourselves? What are the moral and spiritual dimensions of self-responsibility for crafting one's future as a person of color in American society? In sober reflection upon these questions we are reminded by the philosophies of Mary McLeod Bethune, W. E. B. DuBois, Maya Angelou, Gwendolyn Brooks, Malcolm X, and Martin Luther King Jr.—to name only a few— that education is the key.

Brother Malcolm, a champion of truth and self-reliance, puts the matter rather succinctly, "Education is our passport to the future, for tomorrow belongs to the people who prepare for it today."[6] Therefore, the impulse to dream of a better tomorrow must, necessarily, begin with a sense of urgency toward the need for quality education today—as we practice the virtues of self-respect, self-reliance, and faith in God, who gives us moral strength not to quit amid the trials and tribulations of life. Accordingly, the prophet Isaiah affirms a level of faithfulness that literally and symbolically inspires self-esteem. He proclaimed:

[God] gives power to the faint, and strengthens the powerless. Even youths will faint and be weary, and the young will fall exhausted; but those who wait for the Lord shall renew their strength, they shall mount up with wings like eagles, they shall run and not be weary, they shall walk and not faint. (Isaiah 40:29–31)

The principle of self-reliance then is a vital expression of self-esteem. Why? Because the principle itself can move ordinary people of faith to trust in God. Here I think there are two basic points that seem appropriate. First, the moral logic behind this particular biblical text is the wisdom of knowing that God will renew our strength—especially in the heat of struggle for authentic freedom and equality. Second, the moral logic behind this biblical text is the admonition to wait on God.

Some scholars and religious practitioners believe that there are two kinds of waiting: passive and active. Passive waiting, I am suggesting, is prayer without performance. Passive waiting is negative energy on the part of the believer because it means expecting others to do for you what you can do for yourself. It is the failure to recognize that the struggle for authentic freedom and equality is still an unfinished work. Passive waiting means lending voice without vision. It means trusting one's own grit rather than relying upon God's grace.

Active waiting, in contrast, is a prophetic form of communion with God, which moves the human spirit in a new direction. Active waiting inspires within us all a sense of perseverance to keep on keeping on because God is not through with us yet. Therefore, active waiting reinforces the bonds of self-esteem, as it invites the presence of the Holy Spirit, which gives strength to the weak, freedom to the oppressed, and hope to the hopeless and hurting. Active waiting is a form of God's liberating activity in the world that inspires us to feed the hungry and clothe the naked. Brothers and sisters, active waiting is the moral imperative to provide and protect the innocent laughter of our children so that they may grow up in a community without violence and the stigma of racial injustice in America. In short, active waiting is a gift of the liberating presence of God not to give up in the face of adversity and social crisis.

All in all, we can affirm the values of self-reliance and self-esteem as reflected here in the poem "Don't Give Up":

Don't give up
When your bills
Are high,
And your money low
Don't give up.

When your child
Is on crack
And the police on your back
Don't give up.

When a stranger
Prejudges you by
The color of your skin,
Falsely telling the
World that you
Can't win;
Don't give up.[7]

4. Remember always that black history did not begin in slavery, but with ancient Egyptian kings, queens, scientists, sages, and artisans of mother Africa (Genesis 21:9–34, 1 Kings 10:1–13, 1 Peter 2:9–10).

An old Ethiopian proverb reads: "Anticipate the good so that you may enjoy it." Sadly, many African Americans have been led to believe that there is nothing good to anticipate in their own religio-cultural heritage because of the deep psychological scars of slavery. This particular saying may go against the grain of our traditional understanding of the crucibles of black history.

We as humans do not necessarily take comfort in this bold proverbial assertion when it comes to the painful ironies and tragic contradictions of Western history in regard to the plight of people of African descent. I believe that we need to see with fresh eyes the contributions and challenges of black history as a source for building self-esteem and faithfulness in family life.

Years ago I read about a powerful historical writer and literary scholar by the name of Cheikh Anta Diop, who informed many people in America and in our fragile global village about the important contributions of ancient philosophers, sovereigns, scientists, and artists from Africa. Metaphorically, it was as if a new light of knowledge shone brightly in my head for the first time. I moved from a negative rational self, who often echoed from the ghetto streets of our cities the message "Nig—, you ain't sh-t!" to a positive narrative self, proclaiming, "I am somebody! I am a child of God! You may draw a circle and cut me out, but God builds a rainbow to include me in!"

So then, the positive narrative self is grounded in an understanding of life which enables me to affirm what it means to be created in the image of God. Indeed, the positive narrative self is formed by storytelling. The perennial struggle on the part of many of us to move beyond the negative rational self—to claim our true identity as children of God (Genesis 1:26–27)—is a complex issue because of the scars from slavery and white racism in America. The forces of slavery, for example, created not only cultural arguments for the doctrine of white supremacy but biblical arguments as well.

The critical unmasking of the misuse and abuse of the Holy Scriptures can be seen in the biblical narrative of Ham. The so-called curse of Ham argument is a provocative case in point (Genesis 9:25–27). For centuries, this argument has been cited by bigoted writers and some religious leaders to provide biblical justification for the enslavement of black people in the Western Hemisphere. This perverted interpretation of the Scriptures gave rise to the false doctrine of white supremacy in the modern era.

It was Ham's son Canaan, and not Ham himself, upon whom Noah's notorious curse—"A servant of servants shall he be to his brethren"—was cast. It was Canaan, not Ham, who was the traditional enemy of the ancient Israelites. Through the use of the so-called Hamite hypothesis—which was based on the false notion of black inferiority—early European Americans contended that the civilizations of ancient Africa and the Sudan had no culture or religion that white people were obligated to respect.

From this cursory glance at the black–white problems in history, one can observe at least two psychologically tragic consequences in the development of young black youths. First, self-esteem among youths of African descent was lowered largely because of negative portraits and images of Africans as savages, villains, and criminals in the movie industry and mass media. Second, psychological shame arose from the false impression of some black youths that their own history began in slavery.

Parents and youths need to discuss where black history began—with the great kings, queens, philosophers, and artisans of mother Africa. For parents, educators, and all morally sensitive persons, it seems to me that we must provide our youths—black and white together—with better answers than we have done in the past. These issues and others critically impact one's concept of self-esteem and what public schools and churches should be about in the development of all youths regarding the richness and diversity of black history as social forces to overcome what Professor Diop calls a climate of alienation in our world today.[8]

One of Diop's most critically acclaimed volumes is *The African Origin of Civilization,* in which he boldly proclaims, "The ancient Egyptians were Negroes. The moral fruits of their civilization [are] to be counted among the assets of the black world. Instead of presenting itself to history as an insolvent debtor of the black world, it is the very initiator of the 'western' civilization flaunted before our eyes today."[9] He goes on to challenge both scholars and laypersons to remember and claim our rich religio-cultural heritage as well as to restore a sense of historical consciousness to African peoples scattered around the world.

Concerning black esteem in terms of the origin of civilization, Diop further writes:

> Though the hypotheses of scholars often prove true, the fact remains that at the present moment, while awaiting new discoveries to prove the contrary, the sole scientific conclusion conforming to the evidence is that the earliest humans, the very first *Homo sapiens,* were "Negroids.". . . Any Negro type that stands unquestionably at the origin of a civilization is . . . described by the most distinguished scholars as a Negroid or Hamite . . . thus, the first humans were probably quite simply Negritic.[10]

What is at stake here is not the argument among Egyptologists, anthropologists, archaeologists, linguists, or religionists over Professor Diop's attempt to reconstruct African history, but the simple value of knowing—on the part of youths and parents—that black people are included from the very beginning of civilization as full human beings. For example, we may observe in the language and moral tenacity of W. E. B. DuBois that despite the hostile efforts by some bigoted educators and scholars to crush the spirit of blacks and leave out their contributions, we still rise and shine.

5. Do not forget your forebears who once were slaves; who endured the trauma of the Middle Passage; who landed at Jamestown, Virginia, in 1619; and who gallantly fought—by God's grace—to win the prize of freedom from their white oppressors when the Emancipation Proclamation was signed on January 1, 1863 (Deuteronomy 7:7–11, Exodus 20:1–6).

For people with a strong memory of suffering and hope, the subject of self-esteem is exceedingly critical for both children and parents in our time. Self-esteem may be understood in the wider society as confidence and satisfaction in oneself. In the long struggle for freedom, blacks have been compelled by the circumstances of slavery and racial degradation to use their internal strength of self-esteem. What, then, do we teach our children and young adults about the currents of slavery and the Middle Passage? Concretely, we may simply ask, what is meant by the term *Middle Passage?*

According to John Hope Franklin, Benjamin Quarles, and other critically acclaimed historians, *Middle Passage* refers to an unwelcomed voyage over the Atlantic—originating from the home base in Africa—of incredible rigor and danger that slaves were forced to endure. All did not endure the treacherous voyage as human cargo. Benjamin Quarles in *The Negro in the Making of America* has pointed out that, on an average, the Atlantic voyage brought death to one out of every eight black passengers.[11] The concept of the Middle Passage reflects a complex phenomenon which came to be known by some educators and historians as the three-corner slave trade. In 1619 a Dutch frigate attacked a vessel from Portugal and took twenty Africans, who were regarded by the English as beastly savages living without a God, law, religion, or commonwealth.[12] In late August 1619 the Dutch frigate landed at Jamestown with the Africans. Its arrival did not apparently have any immediate impact on the social climate of the colony. But the introduction of this new racial element had extraordinary consequences. For example, the gradual increase of the number of slaves in the workforce in colonial America made the laws of manumission more difficult to enact, and thereby further demoralized the slaves and degraded the quality of black communal life.

Benjamin Quarles, a champion of self-esteem and enlightenment, depicted the whole event this way: "The vessel that sailed into the Chesapeake waters was a privateer, and its coming was as casual and . . . as unexciting as its consequences were far-reaching."[13] The Africans were greedily exploited.

It is only a glimpse into the obvious to suggest that the Middle Passage had important consequences for blacks as it marked the beginning of the Anglo-Saxon–African American experience in the new world. Quarles further provides a lucid description of the Middle Passage:

> When enough Negroes had been procured to make a full cargo, the next step was to get them to the West Indies with the greatest possible speed. Food was stocked for crew and slaves—yams, coarse bananas, potatoes, kidney beans, and coconuts. Then, after having been branded for identification the blacks came aboard, climbing up the swaying rope ladders prodded on by whips. The sexes were placed in different compartments, with the men in leg irons. The ship

then hoisted anchor and started toward the West Indies, a voyage fifty days in length if all went well. This was the Middle Passage, so called because it was the second leg in the ship's triangular journey—home base to Africa, thence to the West Indies and finally back to the point of original departure.[14]

This look at the vicious treatment of blacks in American colonial history underscores the moral strength of self-esteem on the part of people of African descent, people who were able to endure the perilous journey through the Middle Passage. Theologically and ethically considered, self-esteem is a gift of courage nurtured in faith. Despite the trials and tribulations of the Middle Passage, slaves often read the Bible and were secretly instructed by black preachers and some sympathetic whites of the community to "be strong and courageous; do not be frightened or dismayed, for the Lord your God is with you wherever you go" (Joshua 1:9). Thus our children must be taught the hard lessons of self-esteem by riding the wings of courage and faith of those who came before.

As Christians it seems to me that we are always confronted in life with fundamental questions of faith and moral struggle. For example, what is faith? How do we grow wings of faith in black youths today that empower them to see the moral strength of our forebears who once were slaves? What is the role of the church— black and white—in a democratic republic continually marred by racial antipathy and alienation? Can ordinary people with wings of faith make a difference if their wings are untried? When will America unfurl her untried wings of freedom, justice, and equality and soar high for children and adults of African descent? These are the sort of moral questions that the church and persons in contemporary society must agonize over.

For morally sensitive Christians, it is, I think, praiseworthy to note that the Bible teaches us that "faith is the assurance of things hoped for, the conviction of things not seen" (Hebrews 11:1). Faith is not intellectual or schoolbook knowledge, but believing what we cannot prove. It is walking in places where we have not gone and enduring the trials and tribulations of history without being defeated by history. It is basic trust in God that one's untried wings of faith today can find moral strength in our forebears of yesterday who endured the trauma of the Middle Passage. The wings of faith inspire the believer to take seriously the liberating power of God's Word. Faith is a gift from God. In short, faith is not necessarily a gift of reasoning. Cold reasoning alone, for instance, would not have allowed our African forebears to endure the wrongful brutality and cruelty of chattel slavery. Like an eagle soaring high, the wings of faith inspired our forebears to see beyond the human order of social caste and skin color to a divine order of righteousness and inclusivity—where racial difference is not a barrier to our oneness in God. As Scripture affirms, "There is no longer Jew or Greek, there is no longer slave or free, there is no longer male and female; for all of you are one in Christ Jesus" (Galatians 3:28).

6. Chose peace over confusion, righteousness over unrighteousness, and life over death as you walk among the people (Joshua 24:15, Deuteronomy 30:19).

Another important building block of self-esteem is the presence of peace over confusion, righteousness over unrighteousness in the Christian moral life. The struggle, I think, that we have is one of trying to build—morally and spiritually—the sort of values that can create an island of peace within one's soul without negating community. In the midst of the pressures and pains of modern-day life, it is easy in our society to ignore the door within our souls that opens into the presence of God. The hurts and heartbreaks that test the external boundaries of peace often press us, unwittingly, to flee to an internal island of escapism. That is not what I mean by espousing the principle of peace over confusion as a building block of self-esteem.

Indeed, it would be foolish and unwise to suggest to our children and youths of today that to cultivate self-esteem all one has to do is to escape to some lonely island free of the peculiar pressures of drugs, drinking, and drifting. To the contrary, the principle of peace over confusion implies the presence of moral choice. As people of God, our individual lives must reflect that moral choice. We are all involved in decision making, in making choices—big and small, good and evil. We thread our way amongst the throes and conflicts of decision making every day of our lives as we walk amid people in our society. First of all, the principle of choosing people over confusion means that one cannot establish an island of peace within one's soul without naming the evil of racial injustice in the land. Here it seems to me that the language of self-esteem must necessarily involve standing up and naming a particular injustice or abuse.

Ethically I believe that gang violence is an evil we must resist. I believe that reckless teen pregnancy is an evil burden upon our communities, and we must name it that. I believe that dumping and warehousing illegal drugs is an evil burden, and we must name it so. Evil must be named. In a word, without naming there can be no claiming—that is to say, no willingness to accept moral responsibility for one's behavior.

Second, the principle of choosing peace over confusion means that we as parents, educators, preachers, and leaders of the community must remind our children and young adults that true peace is a by-product of justice. By this I mean that the seekers of true peace can disarm the arrogance of power by arming the chariots of justice. The language of self-esteem which must be encouraged in us all simply affirms that without justice in the land, there can be no peace in the human heart. Therefore, it is no accident of history that Martin Luther King Jr., for example, warned the American people about the deeper meaning of peace: "True peace is not merely the absence of tension, but it is the presence of justice and brotherhood."[15]

Third, the principle of choosing peace over confusion means that we rely, ultimately, upon God's power within us to make the right choice. As persons of faith and conscience, we must choose the true God of suffering love over the false god of racial hate. Parents and educators are obligated, for instance, to build bridges of self-esteem in young people by empowering them to resist the gods of seductive peer pressure and embrace the true God of grace and disciplined love who can bring inner peace within one's soul. Inner peace is not the absence of agonizing choices that can bring pain but the presence of God's saving grace that brings power. If you—as a child of God—are still agonizing over where to land on your own island of peace, or where to place your own footprints in the house of worship, the Almighty may be saying, "Choose this day whom you will serve, whether the gods your ancestors served in the region beyond the River or the gods of the Amorites in whose land you are living; but as for me and my household, we will serve the Lord" (Joshua 24:15).

7. Remember that self-love is not the denial of the value of black personhood (Matthew 16:24, Luke 9:23, 2 Corinthians 4:8).

One of the assumptions that I bring to this important discussion arises from the need to articulate a distinctive ethic of self-esteem for African Americans. In recent years, there has been a greater push for accountability in education, economics, religion, and family life with regard to love, faith, and self-worth. Yet the subject of self-esteem is all too often relegated to the narrow interests of psychologists and clinical social workers, who may ignore the biblical and theological foundations of this vital issue.

In an unpublished doctoral thesis entitled "Preaching to Build Self-Esteem in the Local Church Setting," Dr. O'Neal Shyne Jr. boldly asserts:

> Self-esteem, self-love, or self-acceptance seem to traditional Christians to be the opposite of what Jesus said when he declared, "If any person will come after me, let him/her deny himself/herself, and take up his/her cross, and follow me" (Matthew 16:24; Mark 8:34; Luke 9:23). There seems to be little or no awareness of Jesus' declaration that "Thou shalt love thy neighbor as thyself" (Matthew 19:19; 22:39; Mark 12:31). If one takes the Bible seriously, there has to be a way to avoid what, on the surface, seems to be a contradiction. Once this has been resolved, there are many, many passages and various principles which not only accept but require a ministry of self-esteem, to meet the needs of an African American socio-economic group whose view of itself has kept it from complete or even minimal fulfillment of inherent potential.[16]

At first glance, the idea of self-love, from a biblical perspective, may appear to be self-serving and vainly egocentric rather than healthy and natural. Universally I believe that people have a need to feel good about themselves and to find a sense of self-worth as children of the most high God. Unfortunately, there is in the corpus of the Protestant tradition in Western culture the tendency toward ethical dualism. By this I suggest a pattern of social thought inherent in church and society to separate the love of God from the love of neighbor.

For example, the echoing voice of the narratives in both Matthew 22:39 and Mark 12:31 record Jesus saying that the ethical requirements of the Great Commandment involve loving God and neighbor *as self*—not at the sacrifice of self. It seems that Christian faith today clearly supports the notion of self-love—not as unbridled self-indulgence but as a gift we share with others in gratitude for what God has already done for us in Jesus Christ (John 3:16, 1 John 4:19–20)—without the second part of the Great Commandment, which is to love your neighbor *as yourself*. Hence, the principle of self-love—which I think is sorely neglected in the landscape of the African American community today—is not the denial of the value of black personhood.

Undoubtedly the most crucial part in the development of any viable ethic of self-esteem is a healthy concept of blackness. Because of the power of racism in our world, many whites and blacks have negative images associated with the concept of blackness—*black*mail, *black*list, *black* nigguh, *black* sheep, *black* cat, *black* Monday (the day the stock market crashed). The list of negative images associated with the word *black* goes on and on. In short, the concept of what it means to be black must be reinterpreted in light of the positive qualities of the African American religious experience, which will also contribute to one's self-esteem. Theologically, the idea of blackness connotes moral strength that enables one, for example, to affirm that black is beautiful, and it may provide each black child with the courage to overcome adversity in the Christian moral life.

8. Listen first with a heart of love without first judging with a heart of stone the other's action (Luke 23:34, Matthew 7:1–5).

When I was young, I used to watch from the front porch of my home, located in the small rural town of Earle, Arkansas, fellow classmates playing what we affectionately called sandlot basketball. It was a wholesome pastime for all the young boys of the neighborhood. But one day Daniel, a neighborhood kid whom nobody wanted to play basketball with, came to the sandlot court. Under a cloud of doubt and low self-esteem, Daniel felt rejected and emotionally scarred. Of course, Daniel could, in fact, play basketball, and he was as swift as the other boys. As I looked into Daniel's eyes, I saw deep hurt and anguish because my own classmates first judged harshly the actions of another without first seeing with a heart of love.

The moral of this true childhood story is that God wants us to first see with a heart of love the good and self-worth of another human being. One cannot light the fire of self-esteem in young people without gently striking the match against the grain. Although we all have personality quirks, I believe that we must run the risk of striking the match against the grain in order for the exploding light from the Daniels of the world to shine through.

Self-esteem is like a kitchen match in the hearts of young people. Parents, teachers, and community leaders from all walks of life are morally obligated to strike the matches of kindness and curiosity in the minds and hearts of young people. If there is no curiosity, there is no creativity. If there is no sacrifice for the good of our youth, there is no salvation. If there is no humility, there is no heart. If there is no love, there is no life. No cross, no crown. No pain, no gain. No fruit, no future! It seems to me, therefore, that these are the broader lessons of what it means to teach African American youth and others about the power of listening first with a heart of love.

Let us now be practical and ask the question, What does it mean to listen first with a heart of love without judging the other's action? First, Christian faith anchors us in the belief that the struggle of conscience, rooted in love, invites the individual to listen with one's heart. The capacity to listen with one's heart bears witness to the power of God's love inside of us all.

Second, to listen with a heart of love—without prejudging the other's action—means a sober recognition that love is a gift of God. The love in your heart involves reaching out to others; it is a gracious response to the self-giving love found in Jesus Christ, the prime example for the Christian moral life.

Third, Christian faith anchors us in the belief that the true test of love is giving and forgiving the other's action. For example, the New Testament bears witness to the liberating power of love as Jesus whispered from the cross, "Father, forgive them; for they know not what they do." Hence, the capacity to listen with one's heart is morally linked to forgiveness and reconciliation.

9. Throw down ropes from the mountain of success, rather than scissors, so that each person—black or white—might climb (Psalm 30:7, Isaiah 25:6, Exodus 3:12, Mark 15:21).

In the parent–child relationship, I believe in teaching our young people that the mountain of success cannot be climbed based on the credo of rugged individualism. Such a credo says to the child: "I can pull myself up by my own bootstraps. I don't need anybody else because I'm sufficient in and of myself!" During the eighteenth century, it would seem that the Enlightenment story of success and progress became the dominant cultural narrative that most Americans embraced. The two moral dogmas that most Americans turned to were individualism and competition.

Benjamin Franklin and Thomas Jefferson were the best known of the American intellectuals and rationalists who embraced this Enlightenment view of the "Gospel of success."[17] To them, the virtues of the mind were more important than those of the heart; for these two rational individualists, the virtues of reason carried greater weight than faith.[18] That is, the moral traditions of American democracy rooted the concept of self-esteem more in the philosophy of individualism than in the communal spirit. Hence, a child can easily grow in our secular culture with a normative sense of fast-food religion rather than prophetic religion.

In the conceptual framework of the vital principles of self-esteem, one may logically distinguish between fast-food religion and prophetic religion in the child-rearing practices and values of families. Fast-food religion is the religion of individualism and self-indulgence, which may signal to a developing child that in the throes and difficult rhythms of life you can, literally, always have it your way! In the capitalist marketplace of competition and consumption, you can drive to a window and a polite attendant will figuratively say, "May I help you? The fixings are unlimited. Have it your way—mustard, mayo and cheese, but hold the onions!" Fast-food religion is the dominant religion of the marketplace, which promises the child a sky without clouds, the believer a rose garden without thorns, and the young disciple of Jesus a beautiful crown without the agony of the cross.

It seems to me that fast-food religion bears affinity to what Dietrich Bonhoeffer called the dogma of cheap grace—the deadly enemy of our church. Cheap grace means grace without price; grace without cost.[19] In a family or church which holds to the rule of fast-food religion, the young believer is taught a spirituality that does not require moral limits and self-acceptance of responsibility.

Fast-food religion also leads to a privatized faith without respect for moral boundaries between parents and children. A parent, for example, is not given authority by God to be a mere friend to the child. To be sure, a parent must remain a parent, even as the developing child reaches for the esteem of self-actualization and adulthood. Too many well-intentioned but misguided parents try to live like the child, dress like the child, and on occasion act like the child—in order to relate to the child's world. Typically that's a bad mistake for the parent–child relationship, because the parent abandons his or her authority—thereby signaling to the child the fast-food religious message, "Honey child, you can have it your way rather than God's way!"

By contrast, prophetic religion is a religion of *we* consciousness, not the *I* consciousness of individualism. Prophetic religion means coming to terms with the shaping force of a community of love and grace. Prophetic religion means the capacity to live and nurture our children within the limits of responsibility and grace, while serving a God whose grace is limitless. Moreover, prophetic religion is the playground of God's justice and mercy for all peoples of the earth: parents and children, old and young, black and white, the haves and have-nots, the physically challenged and oppressed, and other victims of mistreatment. Prophetic religion means that God sides with the poor and downtrodden of every land, bringing good news to the hurting ones in our midst (Luke 4:18–19). Prophetic religion is the communal sanctuary of God's love where our children can run and hide and find protection from the drug dealers, gang lords, pimps, and pushers of deception and death.

In the widening circle of self-esteem, prophetic religion is expressive of the African proverb, "It takes a village to raise a child." If we rear our children with the moral principle "Throw down ropes from the mountain of success so others, too, might climb," then we may avoid the pitfalls of fast-food religion. To be sure, our children must be taught that prophetic religion begins in the home; it is centered in the compassionate God who loves them and cares for their total well-being: their education and character development, their schools and neighborhoods, their playgrounds and libraries, their friends and foes, and their safety on the street corner as well as their salvation from the church's amen corner!

In short, prophetic religion calls us to embrace a principle of self-esteem inclusive of moral boundaries and the liberating love of God revealed in Jesus Christ. Therefore, we may shout with joy these words from a poem I wrote titled "Lift High the Love of Jesus":

Lift high the Love of Jesus
Above life's troubles on earth;
So parents and children from
Every race,
Will find their
own self-worth.

Lift high the Love of Jesus
In every village and
Every land;
Lift high the love of Jesus
So parents and children, in
work or play, can
take their rightful stand!

10. Remember always that ordinary ability among humans becomes extraordinary under the protective wings of God (1 Corinthians 12:4, Romans 12:6, Matthew 7:11).

In the parent–child relationship, the idea of being under the protective wings of God means something special in the black religious experience. The old wise ones in the black community often advocated a social ethic inclusive of two elements: giving the child roots to anchor the soul in times of adversity, and giving the child wings, so he or she can fly and explore the world of wonderment and mystery. The Bible says that parents must "train up a child in the way he should go" (Proverbs 22:6) and to "remember your creator in the days of your youth" (Ecclesiastes 12:1). Indeed, the principle of ordinary ability strikes a chord in us all. It means that our youths mirror promise. Each child, rich or poor, black or white, is under the protective wings of God. Each child is a sign of God's promise. Each child, regardless of color, class, or rank in the social order, is a precious symbol of the realm of God.

For example, we must always remember how Jesus affirmed the ordinary ability of people as well as warned his disciples against the seduction of arrogance by valuing children as a new paradigm of God's realm: "Let the little children come to me, and do not stop them; for it is to such as these that the kingdom of heaven belongs" (Matthew 19:14).

First, it is a marvelous thing for parents, public educators, and religious leaders of the community to talk with children about the meaning of self-worth as ordinary people in society. By so doing, we instill and model before them the importance of moral and spiritual values in a secular culture. Our children are our future—our benevolent link to the freshness and innocence of humanity.

Charles Dickens expressed it eloquently when he once muttered, "I love these little people; and it is not a slight thing, when they, who are so fresh from God, love us."[20] Undoubtedly, our children are a special sign of God's favor and love. The spontaneity, playfulness, and love that we often observe in children are powerful reminders of what we adults are called to do and be.

Second, in one's strategy for building self-esteem, we are called ethically to be spontaneous without irresponsibility, to be childlike in spirit without childish behavior in moral practice, and to be lovingly playful without playing around. In philosophical ethics, for instance, Aristotle would call these ethical forms beautiful things that participate in one's search for the doctrine of the golden mean in life (that is, a halfway point between extremes). To illustrate the golden mean further, we may say that the virtue of courage is a good thing to develop in our children, yet it must be understood in terms of social balance. In this case, courage is a good thing if, and only if, it is understood as being halfway between bravery and foolhardiness.

Third, it seems to me that one's emerging concept of self-esteem is enhanced by the belief that we all live under the protective wings of God. It is a sobering thought to remind children and adults that God's realm is plenteous and inclusive. For children and parents, it is comforting to know that the love of God is not limited to any one race, religion, class, or nationality. There is no short supply of God's love.

Ethically considered, agape love—which is of God—can change an enemy into a friend because there is no fear in love (1 John 4:18). Agape love can take our ordinary abilities as humans and transform them into extraordinary gifts when they are placed in the hands of God. No one is ever excluded from the transforming power of love—as young and old find refuge under the protective wings of God. All in all, the law of love is the key integrative principle which holds together one's sense of self-esteem and self-worth as a child of God.

Now, to embrace this awareness is a very great thing, or so it seems to me, because it can serve as a clue or building block in the social, moral, and spiritual formation of persons in the global community. Finally, I am reminded in our reflections on how God uses ordinary people to do extraordinary things of what Dr. King said about the durable power of love as a unifying force: "I have discovered that the highest good is love. This principle is at the center of the cosmos. It is the great unifying force of life. God is love. He who loves has discovered the clue to the meaning of ultimate reality."[21]

Open Letter from Father to Son

"Son, learn what I teach you and never forget what I tell you to do. Listen to what is wise and try to understand it."

—Proverbs 2:1–2 GNB

Dearly Beloved Son,

You may not like the words of this letter, but I plead with you to step up to the plate and read them. The words of this letter may not be as exciting to read as soulful rap, but it offers the inquiring mind a practical road map to life. Before you dash out across the field and run your first yard, remember, the best way to commence the journey is with the word God.

My son, you are the chronological category that parents and teachers describe as "young people." Some mean-spirited philosophers often lament, "What a shame it is to waste the golden nuggets of life on the young!" Indeed, the famous Irish writer George Bernard Shaw once remarked, "Youth is a wonderful thing. What a crime to waste it on children." Well, my son, I don't share this view or cynicism about either the virtues or the vices of youth.

Of course your mother, Jasmine-Renée Bryant, and I are still married, but we are not on very good terms. Things go wrong sometimes with adult relationships and people painfully grow apart. This letter is not about us, but about a father-to-son thing. I don't like mixing grown-folks talk with, shall we say, father-to-son talk. So then, I'm more inclined to begin this letter with a piece of advice from the Bible—the source book of wisdom, love, truth, and salvation. While there is no simple, magical formula for obtaining the good life, the Bible is crystal clear about three things pertaining to youth: (1) its affirmation of the vitality and freedom of youth—that is to say, "Rejoice, young man, while you are young, and let your heart cheer you in the days of your youth. Follow the inclination of your heart and the desire of your eyes" (Ecclesiastes 11:9); (2) its affirmation and advocacy of respect for parents and the wisdom of one's elders—that is to say, "My child, be attentive to my wisdom; incline your ear to my understanding, so that you may hold onto prudence, and your lips may guard knowledge" (Proverbs 5:1–2); and (3) its advice to young people to remember the Divine Creator, while in the tender stages of youth—that is to say, "Remember your creator in the days of your youth, before the days of trouble come, and the years draw near when you will say, 'I have no pleasure in them'" (Ecclesiastes 12:1). So then, my son, the right and only place to start in our father-to-son talk is with what I believe to be the best instruction book in the whole wide world: the Holy Bible. The Holy Book is often referred to by Generation X young folks as the Good Book. Well, I believe, my son, that the Good Book is more than a detailed chronicle of religious rap, rather, it is the angels' heavenly story of life's great map. The Good Book tells us more about grace than about grit; it tells us more about the city of Shalom than about living on the streets without a home.

Therefore, my son Buti-Malik Bryant, I write this letter to you because I want to introduce you to the God-force, who gives to each human being on this planet good instructions. And as your earthly father, I am put here on this strangely marvelous but dangerous planet to guide and remind you, my son, that the bare essence of life is to march to the beat of God. You see, Buti-Malik, the deep legacy of the Million Man March was a covenantal reminder that the sons and daughters of mother Africa have gotten out of sync, out of step, out of rhythm to the beat of God. And as I write this letter from my heart, I shall remind you over and over again that *atonement* is just a big fancy word that invites us to get back our right rhythm, that is to say, to march, in the spirit of our African ancestors, to the beat of God.

As your earthly father, I'm here to give you good instruction, so do not forsake my law. As your earthly father, I'm here to remind you, my son Buti-Malik—in a similar manner with my very own daughter, Nikki-Renée Bryant—that despite all the troubles and difficulties that are with us, someone else is also with us, namely, God the beneficent and merciful. Whether in good times or bad, whether in sunshine or rain, whether in harvest or spring, whether at midnight or the crack of dawn, with God the merciful you're never alone. Buti-Malik, I know that these kind of words may be exceedingly hard for you to understand while you're still in the cradle of your youth. But it is precisely because you are still in the cradle of your youth that you dare not forget that you can trust in God the merciful—especially at a time, my son, when so many young African American males are emptying their minds into drinking, drugs, and drifting. Perhaps, this brings us to one of the main points of this father–son letter of concern. The main ethical question in this letter is not, Do I understand the God thing as an African American male living in white America? but rather, Does God care about me as an African American male and believer in Jesus Christ? In American society, we often hear, my son, powerful stories of optimism gushing from the hearts and minds of many Americans. For example, many people say that "youth is the opportunity to do something and to become somebody." They often tell us that "youth is the pleasant spring of life." They echo seemingly the optimist's view that "youth is a period of building up good habits and hopes."

But for the ordinary African American male, life ain't easy. Life is difficult. Life is troublesome. Life is, seemingly, so unfair if you happen to be black trying to survive in America. But the good news, my son, is that you must stand up for yourself in America. Consider the following case in point. Listen up, son. Let me tell you a true story about the value of standing up for yourself. This story involved a slam-dunking competition among my homies. The unfolding of the actual incident is as follows.

My homie June Bug was the biggest bully on the basketball court. We called him June Bug because his head was shaped like a bug—and, of course, he was a bit sensitive about that matter. "I'm gonna crack your homie when you get out here on the sand-lot," shouted June Bug from the center of the court after just devouring the last fellow. My turn was next to face this bully, eyeball to eyeball on center court. When the dust settled, June Bug actually beat me by the score of one point. But I had won a greater victory. You see, I was no longer afraid of this bully. I stood up for myself. And the next time the results were in my favor.

So then, my son Buti-Malik, the critical question is, Does God care about me? By this, I mean to say, Does God care that young black males have the highest rate of violent crime in America? Does God care that 84 percent of most violent crimes against blacks are committed by other blacks? Does God care that black men comprise about 12 percent of the U.S. population, while constituting approximately 45 percent of the federal prison inmates? Does God care that one of the fastest-growing industries in America—the most affluent and technologically advanced nation on this planet—is the prison industry? Does God care that our babies of color die in childbirth more frequently than white or European babies because of poverty and lack of health insurance? Does God care that 50 percent of those who drop out of public high schools are black? Does God care that in this country blacks comprise 46.6 percent of all those arrested for rape, 62 percent for robbery, 39.8 percent for assaults, 31.1 percent for theft, and 29 percent for burglary? With this kind of dismal sociocultural scenario of the state of black life in America, one would be prone to cry in despair, "O God, what's the use of going on in the midst of these funky facts of life?"

Moreover, my son Buti-Malik, I, as an adult and your father, am not blameless. I must take responsibility for my role in this messy, racist, sexist, classist, and spiritually bankrupt society. Although I am black, I too am not guiltless. Son, I atone and I am deeply sorry for not always being there and being able to give to you the three basic things that every American parent ought to be in a position to impart to one's offspring: permission, i.e., the establishment, beginning at home, of moral rules and boundaries for conduct and deciding right and wrong; protection, i.e., the act of being always there for you as a father to guide, instruct, inspire, and shield you from the dangers of what Kenneth B. Clark calls the "dark ghetto" or wherever you may live and dwell; and potency, i.e., the power of being, the freedom to explore, question, and develop the full potential locked up in the genius of your own identity as a human personality.[1]

In one way or another, I confess that I've fallen short in some of these areas. Hold up, if the gods of honesty have their way, I really mean most not just some of these areas. How long and in what form shall I agonize over the state of society that I have left for you to run in the next century? Will society self-destruct as it creeps more rapidly down the seductive roads of relativism and the secularization of social life in America? Will Generation X have any real dealings with the buppie generation or the growing underclass in our society? Is anybody listening to black America, or is anybody just listening to the sounds, cultural rhythms, violent vibrations, and strange signs and happenings in our nation?

Now Buti-Malik, don't turn me off or go off on me for using all this jargon in a simple letter from father to son. Yes, I know that you're only eleven years old and these words perhaps make no sense to you. But bear with me and don't turn me off so quickly. I am simply confessing and trying to say that we as adults have really messed things up badly. We have created a violent society. As adults, we have created a polluted and unsafe environment. We have corrupted the heavens with scrap metal and chunks of toxic waste that fall from the sky upon our heads in countless places and villages from far and near. As a superpower, we have almost unilaterally redefined the boundaries of sovereign authority and political autonomy among the nations of the earth and declared some to be included in the so-called new world order, while the majority of developing nations have been declared "nonexistent" and thereby excluded. We have dismantled welfare and instituted the feel-good policy of voluntarism as the answer for the nation's poor and marginalized.

My son, I tell you this: We have created, in one generation, more funk than the next five generations can wade through. I am dreadfully sorry for my own role in this mess—morally, spiritually, materially—that we have, undoubtedly, left on the shoulders of all the nation's children and grandchildren to bear, ad infinitum. It is no wonder that we need a day of atonement; better still, the nation at large needs a whole year of atonement—from the White House to the drug house, from the pulpit to the pew, and from the amen corner to the street corner of urban life. We are in need of a "new fix" rooted in a stubborn faith that God will not give up on us until we take responsibility for once again creating safe neighborhoods for our children to play in, public schools where teachers can teach and students can learn, and houses of worship where the believers can believe and affirm the liberating power of God's presence in the lives of young black boys who dare to embrace their African heritage.

My son, I know that at the young age of eleven, this letter may feel too formal; it may not make sense to your young eyes; and there are things that you may not fully comprehend because of the limitations of your own childhood experiences as a young African American male. But please read its contents carefully. For in this letter I give you instructions, stories, spiritual principles, and moral values that will serve you well throughout your life and enhance your self-esteem.

From father to son, I want you to know, as you grow older, that you cannot put too much trust in people, your peers, and running buddies. They will often deceive and mislead you. But put your trust in God, who will neither deceive nor mislead you. For as the Bible affirms and reminds us all: "Do not put your trust in princes, in mortals, in whom there is no help. When their breath departs, they return to the earth; on that very day their plans perish" (Psalm 146:3–4).

My son, I want you to know that the key or normative word here is *trust*. When your back is against the wall, when you've nowhere to turn, when your homie just got on your last nerve, don't explode, take a deep breath, chill, and put your trust only in God. That's what this particular Bible lesson is all about. It teaches us—both father and son—that each person can truly trust in a God who "keeps faith forever" (Psalm 146:6); that God shows justice and compassion for the oppressed and people of color (Psalm 146:7); and that God takes pleasure in those folks, including young African American males, who fear, honor, respect, and love the Creator (Psalm 147:11).

From father to son, you can take this particular moral instruction or Bible lesson right to the bank! Notwithstanding, I want you to know, Buti-Malik Bryant, that I—as your father—will at times disappoint you badly. I am only a human being, so frail and vulnerable—and you can't always depend on me. But a truth I give you: you *can* always depend on God.

I vividly recall that when I was your age, God literally saved my life from the waters of death. You see, my son, I once was young just like you. In fact, I was a badass kid, and didn't feel ashamed about it. I was bad as a beast of the forest, or so I thought, for in the dreamland of youth, one thinks many things. There are literally no mountains that cannot be conquered. Well, I am reluctant to admit, but I was silly enough to play with my father's gun. I used to slip it out of my father's bedroom and take the gun into the neighborhood streets to impress my buddies, my homies, my close friends. But one evening I was playing with the gun and went too far and would have been shot had it not been for my guardian angel, my best friend, who saved my life. Oh how stupid, silly, and crazy I was to sneak out my father's gun from our love-filled home to try and pretend I was the new black Rambo on the block!

Well, Buti-Malik, you can see and understand that even fathers and mothers can do and have done stupid and dangerous things in their youth. But I tell you this true story because I love you, and I want you, my son, to avoid doing stupid and dangerous things like playing with guns; becoming involved with gangs, drugs, and drinking and driving; having unprotected sex; acting out uncontrolled anger; and wearing a big chip on your shoulder thinking the world owes you something. My son, all these things can kill you and put you in a grave prematurely.

My son, there are better ways: the way of respect for human life, the way of respect for yourself, and the way of respect for God. God loves you and so do I.

Well, I think it is time to close this letter. Indeed, I've not had the chance before now to be in conversation with you in this manner. You know I cherish the time we spend together—though all too briefly. In the future, I pledge to spend more quality time with you; we still have much to catch up on as father and son. You see, I have confidence in you as a young African American male that you will not let the messy stuff in this society beat you down. Because you are black and a child of God, you are somebody, as our great preachers, teachers, parents, and moral leaders so rightly remind us. Buti-Malik Bryant, my son, you can achieve and soar as far as your dreams and inward faith will take you.

Reachable Dreams

Things are never as hard
As they sometimes seem
If you have reachable
Dreams
Step by step, dreams
Can come true;
It happened to me
It can happen to you.

When tomorrow's plans
Seem impossible
And you are tempted to
Lose your way,
Just ask the Lord
To take control and direct
your footsteps this day.

The Lord God who gave us
His only Begotten Son
Restores the fragments of
Our broken dreams
And gives them back
To us, one by one.[2]

As always, Buti-Malik, I love you very much.

Sincerely,

Your dad

Making Small and Large Differences

WE MUST NOT, IN TRYING TO THINK ABOUT HOW WE CAN MAKE A DIFFERENCE, IGNORE THE SMALL DAILY DIFFERENCES WE CAN MAKE WHICH, OVER TIME, ADD UP TO BIG DIFFERENCES THAT WE OFTEN CANNOT FORESEE.

—Marian Wright Edelman

Today as never before in the history of American society, ordinary people of faith are apparently losing moral ground in the perennial battle against drugs, violence, sexual abuse, marital infidelity, family disintegration, racial bigotry, and spiritual numbness. In rare moments of optimism, the ordinary believer gladly affirms: "God is marvelously present everywhere! Praise God!" But when we see our backs pressed against the wall of adversity, the badge of pessimism around our necks too often reads: "God is present nowhere in the messiness and pain of life! Life sucks!" "Life sucks!" is the dominant echo that resounds in the hearts of many.

Two movements, the Million Man March and the Promise Keepers, have arisen in these pessimistic times. Neither movement is without fault. When I look over the list of virtues and vices often associated with both movements, there appears to be enough moral blame to go around the world a thousand times over. Perhaps the chief fault of each movement, however, is that it seeks to make the big splash, hit the home run, or make the slam dunk.

Marian Wright Edelman is right in saying that the key to progress—both racially and spiritually—is not trying to make a big difference, but rather a small daily difference that "over time, add[s] up to big differences that we often cannot foresee."[1] Perhaps this is the hope or promise, ultimately, that we humans share. Yet individuals and social movements seem to have bold new visions for the cultural and spiritual transformation of a society deeply fragmented by race, gender, and class. But underneath, we see flaws and rough edges in us all.

Put bluntly, a comparative look at the Million Man March and the Promise Keepers is critically needed because things are not always as they appear. The Bible clearly reminds us, "The Lord does not see as mortals see; they look on the outward appearance, but the Lord looks on the heart" (1 Samuel 16:7). Now in terms of understanding the real character or heart of the Million Man March and Promise Keepers, do they constitute a rendezvous of opposites? Let us take a brief look at the habits of the heart that gave birth to an idea, embodied in a college football coach.

The narrative that follows draws upon the distinction often made in feminist ethics and theology between two social constructs on the word *history:* "*his*-story" and "*her*-story."

"*His*-story" of the Promise Keepers

On an ordinary winter day (March 20, 1990), with the promise of spring cracking open upon the horizon, a movement was born. The Promise Keepers did not start out as a movement per se. Rather it started out, apparently, as a simple idea in the minds and hearts of Bill McCartney, former head football coach for Colorado University, and Dr. Dave Wardell—both of whom had traveled to Pueblo, Colorado.[2]

History being partial to irony and surprise, both men found themselves in the vulnerable context of worship and prayer, at which time Coach McCartney posed the crucial ethical question to Dr. Wardell: "What do you feel is the most important factor in changing a man's life spiritually, from immaturity to maturity?" Without pondering the abstract boundaries of Western philosophy and theology, Dave immediately replied: "discipleship."[3]

Bill McCartney went on to share his own ethical view of how there is a special dynamic operative whenever men of faith come together to honor Jesus Christ. Accordingly, what this born-again evangelical coach envisioned was not prophetic criticism of the social structure undergirding a society deeply torn by the demons of racism, classism, and sexism—but rather a sort of internal self-criticism of spiritual numbness that godly men must overcome if we are to have the blessings of family life, church life, and a strong national character. Initially McCartney envisioned a gathering of fifty thousand men at the University of Colorado's Forsom Field in training seminars, or "teach-ins," on what it means to be men of faith, holiness, and moral integrity.

As stated in the booklet *The Ambassador,* Bill McCartney "was imagining a revival among Christian men who were willing to take a stand for God in their marriages, families, churches, and communities. The two elements of revival and discipleship became the foundation and focus of promises."[4]

In March and April 1990, Dave and Coach continued to meet weekly for prayer, strategic planning, and spiritual direction in regard to a large gathering of men. For example, Chuck Lane, who was working with an organization known as Campus Crusade, and Dan Schaffer, who had instructed men for years, weighed in on this idea, and later joined Bill and Dave as the initial core group concerned with spiritual values and the discipline of men on a one-on-one basis. Here emerged one of the models for the core values of the Promise Keepers, namely, the men's small group.[5]

It wasn't until July 1990, however, that seventy-two friends and associates from the core group actually gathered at a local church to discuss the idea of a conference for the men of Colorado. The name Promise Keepers actually evolved from McCartney's speeches to certain churches in Colorado, drawing upon the ethical theme of personal integrity. The ethic of integrity emerged as one of the foundational cornerstones of the movement.

By definition, there were six components identified as descriptive of the credo of integrity on the part of Promise Keepers: (1) utter sincerity, (2) honesty, (3) candor, (4) not artificial, (5) not shallow, (6) no "empty promises."[6] In light of these basic components which comprised the concept of integrity, the organizers sponsored the first conference of Promise Keepers in 1991 by successfully bringing together 4,200 men at the University of Colorado Events Center. Each man who attended the event was challenged to bring twelve others to the following gathering.

A Promise Keeper is committed to honoring Jesus Christ by coming together with others for worship and prayer. And in the candid language of one participant-observer of these initial meetings, "the rest is history . . . right down to capitalizing on their own peculiar version of the Million Man March in October in Washington, 1997. . . . What an irony of American culture!"[7]

Christian Ethics and the Spiritual Journey

Old folks of the religious community out of the Bible Belt lands of the deep South used to have a saying that "everybody talkin' about heaven ain't going there!" I can imagine that part of what they meant stems from the fact that things are not always what they seem or appear. Put another way, the spiritual journey toward forgiveness, wholeness, and reconciliation—which we humans all need—is often marked by tempting parking spaces. The spiritual journey, I think, is not about marches, speeches, accuracy of head counts on the Washington Mall, or the promissory oaths of atonement, but rather, it is all about making a human connection of faith where faith is absent, the will to feel where there is moral and spiritual numbness in families and communities, and the will to be vulnerable to the prophetic criticism of the marginalized and the downtrodden in today's society.

Morality and faith have always been regarded as central to both the Promise Keepers and the supporters of the Million Man March. What the wider community seems to always struggle with is not simply laying bare the etymological roots of the words *morality* and *faith*. For example, it can be argued that the legitimate use of the word *morality* is derived from the Latin word *mos*, from which we get the term *mores*, meaning "manners or customs." The biblical scholar, on the other hand, seems to interpret the word *faith* to mean many things, including: belief in God; trust in the Divine or spiritual things; faith as "ultimate concern" (Paul Tillich); faith as "leaning post" (Rev. C. L. Franklin); faith as "trust or loyalty" (H. Richard Niebuhr); faith as "the assurance of things hoped for, the conviction of things not seen" (Hebrews 11:1); and "faith without works is dead" (James 2:26). Literally the list goes on and on. But the real ethical problem for us as humans—whether a Million Man March participant or a Promise Keeper — is not in proper cognitive awareness or the right definition, but in our concrete living and habits of being in the world.

I contend that the fundamental ethical question among Promise Keepers and participants in the Million Man March is not "What ought I to do?" but the prior issue, "Who ought I to be?" Contextually considered, I propose that the real issue at stake is not political demonstration but moral formation. That is to say, in difficult places where faith connects with the messiness and funky facts of life, the critical question is this: What kinds of persons—Christians or Muslims—are formed as a result of one's suffering and faith claims?

Etymologically, the word *ethics* is derived from the Greek word *ethos,* which means "stall or dwelling" for one's values or moral sentiments. Thus the term *ethos* refers to a web of values or beliefs that function as cement in holding together a community or a society. In short, from a sociocultural perspective, one may simply define ethics as the normative dipstick of the morality and values of a given society and its cultural narratives.[8]

I suspect that notice must be given from the side of Christian ethics that there is a basic difference between Christian ethics and the ethics Christians practice. The two are not synonymous, as seen in our comparison of the Million Man March participants and the Promise Keepers.

From the perspective of methodology, there appear to be two dominant trajectories by which we look at the basic themes, goals, and moral presuppositions of these social movements in contemporary American society. Accordingly, I want to suggest that the Promise Keepers may be characterized by what I call the fundamentalist approach to relating the Bible to Christian ethics, in terms of the moral life. Here a good deal of attention is given to a literal interpretation of those portions of scripture that seem to offer the believer concrete moral commands, injunctions, and authoritative speech, which usually gives the following message: "Brothers in faith, listen up. The Bible is the divinely inspired, perfect Word of God. It means what it says, and says what it means!" For some fundamentalists, the core of this approach can be found in a kind of moralistic reading of the lawlike structure implicit in the Ten Commandments, the Wisdom literature, and the book of

Proverbs. In the New Testament, some fundamentalists emphasize the Sermon on the Mount; parables that deal with patriarchal power; and sections of Paul's letters that address the ethical requirements of women, slaves, and masters (e.g., Ephesians 5:21–28, 6:5–9, Titus 2:9, Colossians 4:9, Philemon 10–19). I must admit that there is no easy ethical equation that can, in fact, provide the reader with a uniform interpretation of these complex passages of Scripture. As an ethicist, what I am concerned about, however, is a creative pattern of moral reasoning that enables us to see more clearly the tensions of power, class, and gender bias built into the fabric of human relationships and systems of faith.

By contrast, if the Bible is indeed to play a role in our reflections and discussion of these two groups, then I would suggest that the Million Man Marchers may be characterized by what some ethicists refer to as a contextualist approach—especially as a remedy for economic powerlessness.[9] By the use of this method of discourse, I mean to convey an understanding of the black experience in America as a concrete source of theology, ethical reflection, and hope for a better future. One of the theological tenets of the contextualist approach—as expressive of the legacy of the Million Man March—is the notion that the God of the Bible takes sides with the marginalized and hurting ones. In this context, the God of the Bible can only be known spiritually and existentially by an oppressed community struggling for freedom and economic empowerment. Because human liberation is a central theme of the gospel of Jesus Christ, the contextualist is concerned with the critical question "What am I to do?" Just as faith, in a functional sense, cannot be separated from "good works" (James 2:17–18), neither can ethics be separated from its theological source, God. That is to say, the reality of God in the mind and heart of the believer is understood and shaped, in part, by the dynamics of the social situation. In terms of their interdependence, the contextualist seems to argue that both ethics and theology reveal a profound interest in the social context in which we live. Thus the theological question "Who is God?" cannot be logically divorced from the contextual question "What is God doing in the world on behalf of the oppressed and hurting ones?" Thus the theological writings of renowned scholars such as James H. Cone in *For My People* and Paul Lehmann in *Ethics in a Christian Context* are powerfully reflective of the contextualist approach to the difficult moral and spiritual problems of life in contemporary American society.[10] By definition, theology is "God-talk" and ethics is "God-walk." But the romance story between theology and ethics does not end there.

At the social level, we must raise the question of not only what ethics is, but what it has to do with the cultural reality of the Million Man March and black suffering in North America. For Christians and secular persons, what has ethics to do with the spiritual crisis of our contemporary culture and the perennial struggle for human liberation? What I am trying to suggest is the basic point that, while the Promise Keepers and supporters of the Million Man March may express a common interest in questions and problems of ethics and theology, they articulate these concerns differently largely because of their particular social, economic, and political location in the dominant American culture. The Promise Keepers seem to favor what I call the fundamentalist approach, while supporters of the Million Man March seem to favor what I call the contextualist approach to the life-and-death issues of morality and faith. With few exceptions, the resounding echo of the Million Man March—beneath the pretentious claims of atonement from the crack of dawn to the dark of night—was the painful reality of white racism! It seems to me that what a good ethic of Christian faith seeks to do is to expose this deadly cancer in the body politic of American culture. As we shall see in our discussion, the Promise Keepers have their work cut out for them, as do those at the Million Man March.

The Bible as Ethical Source

For Promise Keepers and many advocates of the Million Man March, the Bible makes sense because it is the living Word of God, which can inspire acts of atonement and reconciliation among the wounded and marginalized in society. As a normative source of guidance for the moral life, the Bible makes sense because it is a book that gives believers an angle of vision out of which we decide issues of right and wrong and of virtue and vice in our search for the common good. But for Christians, in particular, the Bible is much more than that. The Bible, in the life of the Christian community, is not merely an interesting collection of ancient stories that we may choose to embrace or discard, to like or dislike. The Bible is the redemptive story of God's grace and love for all people on the planet: the "promise keepers and the promise breakers," the high and low, rich and poor, the haves and have-nots, the physically challenged and the gifted, and the voiceless ones in American society. Therefore, to Christian believers, the Bible is a book about us. The Bible is our communal story, but not our possession. To be sure, the Bible is a narrative book that speaks about the redeeming power and love of God, whose center is Jesus Christ, but whose witness can bear fruit for healing and reconciliation for all suffering people. Comparatively speaking, it is precisely here where we may come to see perhaps the logic and irony of the doctrine of atonement in the way the Promise Keepers and participants in the Million Man March use the Bible as a normative source.

Now as an African American male who attended the Million Man March and observed the social dynamics of the Promise Keepers' march on Washington in October 1996, one can easily get the feeling that the Bible—as a source of ethical guidance—seems to be used more to control women and minorities than as an instrument of racial harmony and reconciliation. As ordinary people of faith, we must ponder critical questions: What is the real ethical task before us in our comparative look at the Million Man March and the Promise Keepers in light of their use of the Bible? As black and white Christians who apparently read from the same Bible, what are we called, morally and spiritually, to be and do? In a multiracial and multicultural society, must we have a Bible-toting faith in order to be faithful? Put another way, what kinds of acts are faithful, if we are to establish genuine cross-cultural dialogue? Perhaps, as a normative principle of discourse, the Bible itself reminds us all to "be doers of the word, and not hearers only" (James 1:22).

The fact of the matter is, or so it seems to me, that the ethical task requires that we be genuine in our feelings and dealings with one another. Whether there can be real nitty-gritty dialogue between the men of the Million Man March and the Promise Keepers I cannot say. What I can say reasonably and with passion is that Christians who look at the Bible through the lens of different cultural narratives ought to be in dialogue. I invite you, with the integrity of conscience, to step up to the plate with me and shout:

> Listen up, brotha man . . .
>> we may not be on the same page,
>> but we read and encounter words
>> of suffering and hope from the

same book, from the Holy Scriptures . . .
we may not be successful in
dialogue, but let it be true.
. . . If we fail to establish a
peaceable dialogue, where issues
of justice flourish, can we
expect in America
to really live in peace?

Brotha man in white skin;
. . . I confront you with a bitter
truth that . . . if we—arising from
the bowels of faith and conscience—must
be like ships passing in the night,
let us at least have our
headlights on!

The perennial struggle to envision the ethical task here reminds
me of a poignant story a reporter told several years ago about the
late great Mother Teresa and her passion for the homeless and hurting ones on the streets of Calcutta. She was asked by the reporter,
"Why do you still help the poor and destitute on the streets when
so little seems to change?" Mother Teresa responded gently, "God
does not ask that we be successful; God asks only that we are faithful." I am not sure if genuine dialogue is even possible for people
who have—historically and culturally—lived on different sides of
the tracks in both church and society. I am not even sure, as a person of conscience and moral commitment, if there is the will to
dialogue between men or women from such vastly different
worlds. But I am convinced that the ethical task illuminates what
it means to be faithful over the idol of success in the dominant cul-

ture, where power and racial antipathy seem to sleep comfortably in the same bed!

Therefore, the ethical task involves knowing the pivotal links between what it is in the Bible that informs our faith claims and how we attempt to express them in different cultural worlds, where values and belief systems are in constant conflict.

For Christian social ethics, the Bible remains the normative source and the charter document for the moral life. But the starting point for understanding the ethical task begins with the foundational question "What does an ethicist do?" Out of the critical matrix of faith sharing and biblical interpretation, I think that the job of the ethicist is to try to analyze and understand who and what people are—when they are behaving socially—in light of certain prescribed standards of right and wrong. Accordingly, the job of the ethicist is to normatively reflect on what is, with a keen eye upon what ought to be. For the ones who call themselves children of God, the perceived marriage between "what is" and "what ought to be" is never a simple possibility of logic or conscience. Thus any viable understanding of the ethical task, I contend, must be grounded in the divine indicative rather than the divine imperative. To use the ethical and theological language of Paul Lehmann, the primary question is "What does God do?" The principles of Christian faith teach us that God is active in history: in the particular contexts, stories, experiences, hopes, and struggles of people to make sense out of the tragic contradictions of life. For the moral agent, this God who is active in history is made known through faith in Jesus Christ.

Therefore, discerning the ethical task means knowing the pivotal links between each informing discipline in the life of faith in the church. Therefore, in understanding the ethical task for Million Man Marchers and Promise Keepers, three brief comments seem appropriate. First, understanding the ethical task in the community of faith means speaking the truth about the realities of oppression and the need for divine liberation. With few exceptions, many black theologians and Christian ethicists point out that white scholars and moral thinkers in America have failed to ground their biblical interpretation of the human predicament in an analysis of God's liberating activity. It seems to me that the burden of the ethical task is to speak the truth about the role of ethics in the contemporary American scene and its tendency to separate the politics of God from the politics of racial oppression. Second, the burden of the ethical task involves nothing less than speaking the truth to power. "For our struggle is not against enemies of blood and flesh, but against the rulers, against the authorities," says St. Paul (Ephesians 6:12). Third, understanding the ethical task involves speaking the truth with love.

The norm of love is the highest virtue of Christian faith. But for the Christian community, it is a virtue whose faithfulness is legitimated by doing justice, feeding the hungry, clothing the naked, and caring for the poorest of the poor, as in the life exemplified by Mother Teresa. The task of speaking the truth with love aims at the establishment of justice and righteousness on behalf of the poor and oppressed in the land. Jesus reminded his disciples that love must be the motivation of moral action. He asserted, "Love the Lord your God with all your heart, with all your soul, with all your mind." In short, the individual who is faithful to the ethical task discerns the close connection between love and the struggle for justice and peace.

Let us now turn to some of the particular faith claims or biblical pronouncements made on the part of those who follow the moral teachings of the Promise Keepers. Although the Promise Keepers have been sharply criticized by feminist and liberal religious groups of the political left, let us take a comparative, though brief, look at the specific biblical principles and moral commitments that they espouse in reaching out to men of color in American society. These biblical principles include the following affirmations embodied in their Statement of Faith.

1. We believe that there is one God eternally existing in three persons: the Father, the Son, and the Holy Spirit.

2. We believe that the Bible is God's written revelation to man and that it is verbally inspired, authoritative, and without error in the original manuscripts.

3. We believe in the deity of Jesus Christ, His virgin birth, sinless life, miracles, death on the cross to provide for our redemption, bodily resurrection and ascension into heaven, present ministry of intercession for us, and His return to earth in power and glory.

4. We believe in the personality and deity of the Holy Spirit, that He performs the miracle of the new birth in an unbeliever and indwells believers, enabling them to live a godly life.

5. We believe that man was created in the image of God, but because of sin, was alienated from God. That alienation can be removed only by accepting through faith God's gift of salvation which was made possible by Christ's death.[11]

Descriptively, the theological framework implicit in this Statement of Faith is fundamentalist and evangelical in character. With a sense of radical intentionality and religious fervor, they propose a "Christ-centered ministry" dedicated to the moral disposition of uniting men from all walks of life—regardless of race, class, culture, economic status, or geographical location into a kind of "brotherhood of biblical reconciliation." This male-oriented ministry of outreach, as their promotional literature affirms, means "loving our brother as an expression of our love for God" (1 John 4:19–21).

The Promise Keepers contend that they are not concerned with short-term results but rather a lifelong commitment to a personal relationship with God, to family, to fidelity in marriage, and to godliness in matters of Christian conduct. Accordingly, a Promise Keeper is committed, in principle, to the following seven promises:

1. Honoring Jesus Christ through prayer, worship and obedience to His Word, in the power of the Holy Spirit;

2. Pursuing vital relationships with a small group of men, understanding that he needs brothers to help him keep his promises;

3. Practicing spiritual, moral, ethical, and sexual purity;

4. Building strong marriages and families through love, protection, and biblical values;

5. Supporting the mission of his church by honoring and praying for his pastor and by actively giving his time and resources;

6. Reaching beyond any racial and denominational barriers to demonstrate the power of biblical unity;

7. Influencing his world, being obedient to the Great Commandment (Mark 12:30–31) and the Great Commission (Matthew 28:19–20).[12]

Now a comparative look at the day of atonement in commemoration of the second anniversary of the Million Man March reveals a process by which Minister Louis Farrakhan strongly encouraged people of color to come together. While Farrakhan, the controversial leader of the Nation of Islam, has had words of praise for Promise Keepers in the noble effort to call men back to

God, the ethical burden of fairness in the public sector of society was not the same when it came to black men. Comparatively speaking, Farrakhan pointedly said to a gathering in St. Louis: "But when I called African American men to come together, the opposition accused me of gathering an army."[13] Notwithstanding, the esteemed leader of so many young African American males went on to touch a conciliatory fiber in the body politic of a fragmented culture by proclaiming, "If a million black men and a million white men would come back to God, then we can make some changes in this nation. Anything that pulls men back to God is a noble thing."[14]

I think, as an ethical theologian and black male, that it is not easy for men of color to talk about racial reconciliation, healing, and coming back to God. Why? Because the memory of oppression and racial degradation is so long in American history and the agonizing pain of racism is so fresh in the body politic of the dominant culture. Yet we are our brother's keeper along the road toward racial reconciliation, genuine dialogue, and healing. Hence arises this journey toward healing the land and spiritual unity that Farrakhan described as a process involving at least eight steps to atonement.[15] These steps of moral guidance are expressive of the following elements:

1. Pointing out the wrong—Making a diagnosis.

2. To acknowledge—To admit the reality or truth of the fact that you are wrong.

3. To confess—To relieve the soul of guilt. Only through confession, we are granted protection against the consequences of our fault.

4. To repent—To feel remorse when you confess to God (first) then to the person(s) whom your faults have ill-affected.

5. Atonement—To do something to correct your faults. To bring about satisfaction or reparations for a wrong or injury.

6. Forgiveness—To ask and to grant pardon for evil or sin. To cease to feel resentment to the offender (to liberate).

7. Reconciliation—To resolve differences. To become friendly and peaceful again.

8. Perfect union—A healing.[16]

From a comparative perspective, I think that these eight steps to atonement are important touchstones in building up the spirit of the community and creating a social and moral climate for cross-cultural dialogue. For example, many social critics and supporters alike of the Million Man March are often quick to point out that during the month following the historic October event in 1995, the largely poor urban communities in our nation experienced a drop in crime, drug use, homicide, and gang-related violence. Sociologically, it would be premature and irresponsible to declare the "dawn of a new society" as a result of Minister Farrakhan's initial call for a national day of atonement. But as an attendee of the March, I can reasonably say that I observed a change in attitude of black men from St. Louis toward their families and neighborhoods upon returning home. Some social workers even reported an increase in the adoption of young black children as a possible result of the Million Man March—as it called for a sense of social responsibility and atonement in the bleak ghettos of our nation.

Together, yet Divided

Despite the noble call for reconciliation and healing on the part of the Promise Keepers and the attendees of the Million Man March, there is still the "great divide." It has always been there, from the beginning of U.S. history, as the first slave stepped off the boat from Africa, emotionally torn from his children and family, snatched from his native village of security and familiarity, enchained by European greed and lust for power, and sent across the Atlantic in the stench of fear and death, lodging in the belly of countless slave ships on the way to a strange new world. It is in the power of this great divide, set off by centuries of oppression and moral degradation, that we speak openly and honestly about the "promises" of the Promise Keepers in light of the spirit and legacy of the Million Man March.

I agree with the sober observation of Nibs Stroupe and Inez Fleming, in their acclaimed book *While We Run This Race,* that "we have come to a watershed on race relations in this society. We all had hoped that we had overcome, but we have not. Many of us are surprised . . . that we have returned to this great divide.[17]

Despite the tremendous gains of the civil rights movement of the 1950s and 1960s, we still hear this echo of the great divide at the dawn of a new century—as expressed in the growth in segregation of the nation's public schools, the forced integration of an all-white housing project in Texas,[18] or California's Proposition 209 and the subsequent dismantling of affirmative action.

As a Christian believer and African American male, I am deeply concerned and dismayed that cases like these continue to characterize race relations today—as they contribute to mistrust, racial antipathy, and the widening of the gap between black and white, the haves and the have-nots in American culture. Even in the household of faith, for example, the Promise Keepers represent not the noble ethical exception but the rule. As a conservative evangelical group, they purport to bring all men together under the banner of Jesus Christ and the doctrines of salvation and racial reconciliation; but the fact of the matter is that 96 percent of the Promise Keepers are white males. I am simply trying to say this:

despite important signs of black progress in education and economics over the last two decades, race has been an American obsession and it is still symbolic of the great divide. Andrew Hacker, in his book *Two Nations,* underscores the pervasive shadow of race in American culture:

> Black Americans are Americans, yet they still subsist as aliens in the only land they know. Other groups may remain outside the mainstream—some religious sects, for example—but they do so voluntarily. In contrast, blacks must endure a segregation that is far from freely chosen. So America may be seen as two separate nations. Of course, there are places where the races mingle. Yet in most significant respects, the separation is pervasive and penetrating. As a social and human division, it surpasses all others—even gender—in intensity and subordination.[19]

From the perspective of Christian ethics, I agonize over the fact that the echo of the great divide rings loud in the body politic of the whole church today as some Promise Keepers seek to reach out to their brothers of the Million Man March over the chasms of color, class, gender, denominationalism, and sexual orientation.

For example, the metaphor of a doorbell is interesting in our reflections upon the racial factor in the religious community of faith. When the doorbell rings in our racially divided society, we never know who will be there. We are either pleasantly surprised or racially fearful at the sounds and murmurings from the other side of the door. Do we pretend that no one of importance is there as we hear the echo of the knock from within?

In moments of spiritual musings and the gentle tug of conscience, can we imagine that the echo from the doorbell may be the sound of an Asian? a Latino? a Native American? a Jew? an African? a Russian? a European? a physically challenged person? a gay or lesbian? a sage or sinner? a friend or stranger? or a person of color propelled by the power of a million women holding hands and feeling the energy of sisterhood and self-respect—in Philadelphia, the "City of Brotherly Love"—on a historic rainy day in October 1997? Here it is a glimpse into the obvious to wonder who will answer when the doorbell rings in our racially divided society. Metaphorically, who will welcome the stranger from the other side? Who is the stranger?

Although symbolically turning to men of color with an olive branch of reconciliation, the hard ethical question is this: Can Promise Keepers build a bridge sufficiently over the great divide to welcome strangers who seem to demand more than a mere day of atonement in our nation's capital, who demand a day of justice? Again, it seems to me ethically that when we ring a doorbell, it asks the question, "May I come in?"

Brothers and sisters, do we not remember and hear the echo of inclusion and spiritual connectedness as affirmed by God in the Holy Scriptures: "Listen! I am standing at the door knocking; if you hear my voice and open the door, I will come in to you and eat with you, and you with me" (Revelation 3:20). Because there is no bell like the doorbell of freedom in a democratic society, blacks and other marginalized people who have struggled and felt pain have labored for inclusion at all levels of life in the American sociocultural system.

This particular point brings us face to face with three domi-nant flaws in the religious and moral value system of the Promise Keepers in society today. First, there is the flaw or danger of sex-ism implicit in their biblically based but fundamentalist theology, which tends to mesh neatly with the rhetoric of right-wing political leaders, who glamorize "American family values" and the "traditional roles" of women as homemakers as normative at all levels of society. For example, why not allow women to freely attend meetings and fully participate in the organizational structure and decision-making process of the Promise Keepers?

Second, I must admit, as an African American male and religious scholar, that I find a bit suspect a mass movement of European American white men, who claim some divine moral mandate or inspiration to invite their "lowly, spiritually deprived" black brothers into their religious ranks under the banner of Jesus Christ. Here it seems to me that there is a profound aura of religio-cultural paternalism in the Promise Keepers. To be candid, I question their motives; and I must raise the hard ethical question "Are they for real in their knee-jerk gestures toward racial harmony and peace?"

Third, I am suspicious of any religious group that seems to degrade women as equal partners in God's scheme of human creation and the tendency to stereotype young black men as gangsta rappers, muggers, violent criminals, and lazy misfits of the ghettoes of America. Ethically I think that what is at stake here in our discussion of the Promise Keepers, as a religious group, is the perennial moral struggle, as a follower of Jesus Christ, to look beyond the spiritual rhetoric to the harsh social reality of growing up black and male in a predominantly white racist society.

Now, while the Promise Keepers have focused in part on the real need of men to have a spiritual connection with God as the Creator, their social praxis or the "habits of the heart"—to paraphrase the eminent sociologist Robert Bellah—still look suspiciously white. In an ideal world of cultural harmony and religious reconciliation, most morally sensitive persons would love to hear the Promise Keepers shout, "Come on in, brothers and sisters.

The trumpet of justice and the doorbell of freedom have sounded, and all are welcome to feast equally at God's table of peace and mercy, regardless of race, religion, class, gender, sexual orientation, or occupational location in the socioeconomic system in the U.S." But the sad case of a society handed down to us by the social forces of history is that we don't live in an ideal world. In North American society, the fabric of our social world is full of the messiness and funky smell of black and white.

Both Promise Keepers and Million Man Marchers are together, yet separate. Ironically, while we run this race under the U.S. flag of freedom and democracy, we embrace a public faith in a common future; yet "we have come this far by faith," as an old Negro spiritual says, but not from a common past—having been tattered and torn by unmerited suffering and racial oppression and forced to come up a different side of the mountain trying to get home. Therefore, the American obsession with race, since the first time Europeans sighted "savages" on these shores, has contributed to our sense of alienation and the burden of conscience in regard to the great divide.

Out of pride and racial hypocrisy, many Promise Keepers seem to ignore the hard facts of our cultural reality in regard to the economic workplace among professionals in our society. For example, we Americans—Christian and non-Christian alike—seem to eagerly advocate a color-blind society of equal opportunity and inclusion for all people. But a cursory glance at the hard facts reveal a different view of the nation's racial health:

- Of U.S. airplane pilots, 98.3 percent are white.
- Of U.S. geologists, 95.9 percent are white.
- Of U.S. dentists, 95.6 percent are white.
- Of U.S. authors, 93.9 percent are white.

- Of U.S. lawyers, 93.8 percent are white.
- Of U.S. aerospace engineers, 93.8 percent are white.
- Of U.S. economists, 91.9 percent are white.
- Of U.S. architects, 90.6 percent are white.[20]

This information, gathered from the Federal Bureau of Labor Statistics, reveals a configuration of racial and ethnic patterns of progress in wider society ignored by the Promise Keepers.

W. E. B. DuBois, in his classic *The Souls of Black Folk,* captures the bitter irony and hope of today's African American—male or female:

> The Negro is a sort of seventh son, born with a veil, and gifted with second-sight in this American world,—a world which yields him no true self-consciousness, but only lets him see himself through the revelation of the other world. It is a peculiar sensation, this double-consciousness, this sense of always looking at one's self through the eyes of others, of measuring one's soul by the tape of a world that looks on in amused contempt and pity. One ever feels his twoness,—an American, a Negro; two souls, two thoughts, two unreconciled strivings; two warring ideals in one dark body, whose dogged strength alone keeps it from being torn asunder.[21]

Although this classic formulation of the American dilemma was constructed nearly a century ago, the genius of intellect still struggles today with the task of unmasking the meaning of one's "twoness and double consciousness." Historically considered, one's consciousness of the great divide did not start with the emergence of the Promise Keepers on the contemporary American scene.

For example, Alexis de Tocqueville, the distinguished French writer, was keenly aware, as a social analyst and observer of American cultural patterns, of the significance of race. He observed that race was a bedrock pillar of the religio-cultural value system in American society. The perpetual anxiety over race is a continuing refrain in economics, law, politics, public education, private industry, science, and religion. In short, race is the dominant thread—for better or worse—around which we order the cultural fabric of our common life in the United States.

From ethical and theological perspectives, I think that we inadvertently breed and nurture race consciousness in America—whether we are Promise Keepers, Million Man Marchers, Bible-toting Christians of the religious right, or liberal agnostics of the political left. The point is, race matters in America. Race is a decisive center of values in the normative culture. It is a critical point of orientation and redefinition of identity beyond the doctrinal beliefs and moral claims of American Christianity. For instance, the blatantly prejudiced portraits and racial stereotypes of the African American as "little black Sambo," "mammy," "welfare queen," and "uppity nigger" seem to underscore the extent to which certain folks in this country will go to put down and demoralize its own citizens of color.

The irony of race, this peculiar pattern of double consciousness inflicted on the vulnerable identity of the black person, is cogently described by C. Eric Lincoln in *Coming through the Fire:*

> In America, race is the touchstone of all value, the prism through which all else of significance must be refracted before relationships can be defined. . . . There is no order of reality large enough to transcend its pervasiveness, small enough to escape its intrusiveness, or independent enough to avoid its imprimatur.[22]

The ethical riddle of race in America will require, if history is not to repeat the tragic deeds of the past, more than a day-long prayer vigil by Promise Keepers on the virtues of forgiveness and racial reconciliation. We need to recognize that race is a fly in the soup of American democracy. Indeed, the future health of our democratic republic is seriously threatened by this unsavory fly. I am reminded of the famous words of James Weldon Johnson, who once remarked that "the race question in America involves the saving of the black America's body and the white America's soul."[23]

Steps toward Common Ground

Women from all over America—undaunted by rainy weather or the cold pavement of city streets—marched in Philadelphia on October 25, 1997, in celebration of sisterhood, human dignity, and spiritual renewal in the community. A week prior to this Million Woman March, I broke away on October 16 from my regular routine and class schedule at Eden Theological Seminary (where I teach Christian ethics) in order to participate in the local events commemorating the second anniversary of the Million Man March under the shadow of the Gateway Arch in downtown St. Louis. The stronger-than-expected turnout of women, in solidarity with the brothers, evoked my heart and soul to recall the old African proverb, "It takes two hands to play the drums!"

We may say that one hand reminds us of the small steps that both women and men of color have taken together throughout the history of the United States in the long tedious struggle for freedom, justice, and equality. The other hand is the hand of God—guiding, sustaining, and empowering us as we journey along the way, seeking common ground in the absence of common ground, seeking justice in the eclipse of justice under the perilous shadow of Proposition 209, and seeking the remnants of faith in a faithless system of public education, housing, and welfare that seems to strip our children and young people of their dignity, respect, and safety. Yet the mighty hand of God continues to play out new rhythms, in search of common ground amid the uneven drumbeats of our lives.

We as moral agents and as men and women of faith are faced with the burden of ethical decision making. For example, as someone who attended and was inspired by the Million Man March, I find myself pondering these questions: What kind of ethical decision leads one to attend the Million Man March, or for that matter, the Million Woman March? What is an ethical decision in regard to small steps toward common ground? I think that as a people of God, these are important questions as we face the moral and spiritual challenges of a new century. As sojourners of faith and moral struggle in this land, we live more by the fragile movement of small steps than by giant leaps of faith.

We need to grapple with the perennial question "What is an ethical decision?" if we are to better understand the legacy of the Million Man March and what common link, if any, it has to the Promise Keepers. Now concerning a functional definition of the term *ethical decision,* we may simply say it is a choice made, big or little.[24] Indeed, I would suggest to the reader that the very character of the ethical implies the presence of choice on the part of the moral person. Put another way, the burden of the ethical means that God has endowed each human person with the mental faculty to choose, to affirm or reject, and to decide morally the critical issues at stake in life. On this point, the Bible seems to be crystal clear. The story of Joshua bears witness to a decisive faith in God by declaring: "Choose this day whom you will serve, whether the gods your ancestors served in the region beyond the River or the gods of the Amorites in whose land you are living; but as for me and my household, we will serve the Lord" (Joshua 24:15).

I think that it is only a glimpse into the obvious to suggest that in the lived world of experience, an ethical decision constitutes a moral choice. For it is in contrast to an "immoral" or "unethical" decision to make sense out of the human predicament in one's inner struggle. For example, when Rosa Parks decided on December 1, 1955, in Montgomery, Alabama, to sit at the front rather than the back of the bus, she turned a little decision into a big one—that inevitably started a social revolution in a segregated society.

When Martin Luther King Jr. decided to lead a march in our nation's capital on August 28, 1963, he was turning a little decision into a big one, which resulted in the historic Civil Rights Act of 1964, signed by President Lyndon B. Johnson. The bill, which guaranteed access to public accommodations, was previously submitted to Congress by President John F. Kennedy. But it took the act of courage and conscience on the part of Martin Luther King Jr. to declare, "I have a dream!" Indeed, it is reasonable to assume that for a people whose faith is grounded in a God of justice and love, a solitary act of conscience can transform a nation. A little decision becomes a big one when placed in the hands of God.

When nine brave African American students in 1957 decided to attend the all-white Central High School in Little Rock, Arkansas, their small acts of courage set into motion a new philosophy of public education in this culture. As moral agents, therefore, our own life story or ethical stance may not be as dramatic as these historic cases, but the mere act of decision making always implies a choice made for good or evil, for selfish purposes or noble ones.

We now come squarely to the critical moral question, Is there common ground between the Promise Keepers and men of color in our struggle to make sense out of the gospel of Jesus Christ and the promise of racial reconciliation? This is a difficult question for me, ethically and theologically, because of our different cultural narratives in U.S. history. On the one hand, black people's faith in God has enabled us, through the long night of weary years and silent tears, to survive the evils of racism and white male dominance in the United States. Yet the burden of the ethical demands more than mere survival by Christian men and women of faith. It demands the actualization of God's freedom on behalf of the oppressed and hurting ones in our midst.

The reason the question cannot be answered—as a simple possibility of moral discourse—is because black men and white men may read from the same Bible, but they live in different worlds. The social context of their strivings for meaning, purpose, and the good life reflect a different road traveled. It seems to me that black men and white men, in large measure, have lived on different sides of the tracks, and have, in their spiritual and cultural strivings, come up on different sides of the mountain in response to the moral imperatives of the Bible.

For example, mothers and fathers of the black religious experience often give testimonies by proclaiming, "We have come this far by faith" or "We've come up the rough side of the mountain tryin' to get home!" Therefore, on one level, for a people with a deep history of misery and oppression, the only sure promise that oppressed blacks want from the Promise Keepers is authentic freedom. Theologically, I find courage in the contention that if black men and white men are to find common ground in the gospel of Jesus Christ, that gospel, which grows out of God's suffering love for all humanity, must mean freedom. "For freedom, Christ has set us free" (Galatians 5:1). What, then, is the basis of our hope for common ground ethically and biblically? I would modestly offer the following small steps as ethical connectors in the search for common ground between men of color and the Promise Keepers.

- All people—male and female—are made in the image of God (imago Dei), and we all stand in need of God's grace (Genesis 1:26–28).
- We all need forgiveness and healing because of sin and brokenness (Romans 6:20–23).
- We all need a sense of atonement that ends in spiritual empowerment and reconciliation (Romans 5:10–11).
- We all stand in need of God's abiding love because of sin—as the struggle for power is unceasing (John 15:10).
- To love God, do justice (Micah 6:8).
- When others plot, God plans, hears, and delivers us from all fears (Psalms 34:4–7).
- Prayer means not losing hope and trusting God, who shows us the river of life (Revelation 22:1–7).
- Spiritual connectedness or wellness begins with me (that is, telling my faith story or refusing to remain silent) (Matthew 5:14–15).
- To be spiritually alive, be social transformation oriented (Romans 12:1–2).
- As human beings before God, we are more alike than different (Galatians 3:28).

Finally, I submit that these are small steps or normative guides seeking common ground between the Promise Keepers and men of color. We would do well to remember, being honest to God and ourselves, that as humans with feet of clay we don't always get it right. Thus we must stand forever in the spirit of humility and divine grace, whether in the evangelical ranks of the Promise

Keepers or promise breakers; we stand in the shadow of God's suffering love and grace with the sober recognition that God as revealed in Jesus Christ is not finished with us yet. In short, the world's greatest need today is the need of morally honest persons or Christians who can truly say, "God makes a difference in my life! Jesus and I are friends!"

The only conditions of friendship with Jesus are love, trust, surrender, and the integrity of conscience as women and men of faith seek a common place of dialogue and vulnerability. Nothing more is required. Nothing less is tolerated. Brothers and sisters of faith and moral struggle, when you hear people say, "I belong to Jesus," that is an affirmation that moves beyond a mere testimony in the house of God; it also symbolizes a "friendship thing." In one's head and heart, it is an affirmation that says, "Jesus is my big brother."

I've got the best
Big Brother of all
He is handsome and tall;
He helps me when
I am about to fall.
Some say, "He is my
All and all!"

I've got the best
Big Brother of all,
He makes me feel
Great when others
Snap, "You are small!"

I've got the best
Big Brother of all,

In the heat of battle
Upon him I
Can depend;
He'll be with me
To the end.

So, why be anxious
By raising a big fuss
He has already promised
To be with us.[25]

Open Letter from Father to Daughter

FATHERS, I THINK, ARE MOST APT TO APPRECIATE THE EXCELLENCE
AND ATTAINMENTS OF THEIR DAUGHTERS; MOTHERS, THOSE OF
THEIR SONS.

—Tryon Edwards

Dearly Beloved Daughter,

I am writing this letter to you out of the deep river of my own soul. At times I know I have behaved more like the irresponsible dude on the block than the father who is solid as a rock. This letter is not easy for me to write because I have problems putting my feelings down on paper. The river in my soul runs so deep for you and your well-being, the banks of the river cannot contain its mighty currents. So my beloved, be patient with your father as I try to express my conflicted feelings, pains, emotions, agonies, anxieties, desires, and dreams that are locked up in the deep river of my soul. You see, my child, my relationship with your mother has been an on-again, off-again affair.

I am ashamed and I confess that I have not been a good father for you. You see, my daughter, I believe that a good father is not an absentee landlord from the home. I confess that I have, indeed, been absent from your life. Strangely enough, I've been around certain times of the month. I peep and oftentimes look in on you, while you gently recline upon a pillow of sleep at night. Yet I've been absent from the ordinary details of your daily existence: the laughter and sadness, the play and work, the favorite foods and drink, your friends and playmates, and, above all, your dreams and fears. During most of these youthful occurrences and happenings, I plead guilty as an absentee father. But I do care! And I do need to step up to the plate and be a real father rather than the old dude who haphazardly shows up, sometimes once a month or every other month to try and make amends with your mama. In expressing my true feeling, I guess I'm trying to say, daughter, that I wanna be the real dad—the dad I never was.

Nikki-Renée Bryant, you are so young, only seven years old, but in your eyes are the dreams and hopes of a mighty race. My daughter, did I ever tell you about the great women of color who beat the odds of black suffering and putdown in white America? Did I ever tell you about their toils and struggles? Did I ever tell you about their stories of courage and character? Did I ever tell you about the wounds of slavery and how our people were knocked down but not out? Did I ever tell you about the slave ships that were no match for the "ole ship of Zion"? Did I ever tell you about your grandma's Jesus and your grandpa's God? Well, Nikki-Renée, let me reason with you. I can't tell it all, and I probably won't get the whole story straight, but I'll tell you, my beloved, as much as I can remember and what was told to me. You see, Nikki, our journey in America has always been a journey of love and conflict as a proud people of African descent. Love and conflict symbolize the two poles upon which our strivings and musings, our triumphs and tragedies, and our personal and social experiences rest. Love and conflict are the core boundaries of human existence; they tell us what is at stake as we live, move, and have our being in the world. So then, Nikki-Renée, did I ever tell you, for instance, about the toils of Phillis Wheatley, who beat the odds of black suffering and slavery? Phillis Wheatley was born into slavery in 1754. At the tender age of seven she was sold in a Boston slave market to John Wheatley. Being graciously treated as a member of the family, young Phillis was taught to read and write, given religious instruction, and encouraged to read widely in classical literature, philosophy, and the Bible. She became an outstanding poet and an advocate for freedom. In 1773 she was given her freedom after many bouts with poor health. She and Nathaniel Wheatley traveled to London, where she was received as an honored guest by the Countess of Huntington and enjoyed the company of those who fought against slavery.

My beloved daughter Nikki-Renée, I tell you something about the courageous story of Phillis Wheatley because she was seven years old, just as you are now, when she was sold into slavery. Though physically frail, she beat the odds of slavery and adversity in her day. But in America now, my daughter, you have a different kind of slavery. Nikki, it is only a glimpse into the obvious, my child, to say that you are in a new form of slavery. I weep deeply for you as the river of my own soul runs dry. I dread to think about the seemingly insurmountable odds you will face in contemporary American society. As a child of color, you must fight the slavery of drugs; you must fight the slavery of abuse; you must fight the slavery of gang violence; you must fight the slavery of child molestation; you must fight the slavery of poverty; and you must fight the slavery of neglect and cruelty while growing up black in America. The dreadful list of enslavements seems never to cease; I can't protect you from all of these means of enslavement.

If I would be absolutely honest with God and you, I may be the source of some of your pain and the burdens you will carry as you grow older and confront the challenges of adolescence, the teen years, young adulthood, and the full blossom of womanhood. Though I weep inside for you, I also pledge my love to be there for you. It may not always be a physical thing, but it shall never be invisible or absent from the river of my soul. Whether I am present or absent, just remember that you, like Phillis before, can beat the odds. Never quit! Never give up! Never abandon the dreams of your heart! And what I must say, though reluctantly and fearfully, is *"Never* give up on your daddy because God ain't finished with me yet—for God's finger is still stirring in my pot!" Nikki-Renée, I want you to always remember the skillful toils and graceful literary rhythms of Phillis Wheatley, who embraced the Divine by mingling the sacred and secular toils of life under the yoke of slavery into a single statement of dignity and redemption. One can see the expression of this concern in her classic poem "On Being Brought from Africa to America":

> 'Twas mercy brought me from my *Pagan* land,
>   Taught my benighted soul to understand
>   That there's a God, that there's a *Saviour* too:
>   Once I redemption neither sought nor knew.
>   Some view our sable race with scornful eye,
>   "Their colour is a diabolic die."
>   Remember, *Christians, Negroes,* black as *Cain,*
>   May be refin'd, and join th' angelic train.[1]

O my beloved daughter, just imagine this. You're born in another place—on a stately plantation on the outskirts of Boston. It was the customary practice of the nation to think of African slave girls as good fundamentally for two things in the stoic world of Puritan culture: domestic work and sexual pleasure at the capricious will of the slave master. The year is 1761, and the smell of liberty is gradually growing stronger like fragrance after the rain. You're a bright but frightened and fragile seven-year-old child forced by fate and the cruel ironies of U.S. history to stand at attention like a wooden solider before white colonial traders to be sold on the Boston market to a strange family.

O Nikki-Renée, just imagine the quiet whispers, harsh words, and disrobing looks that must have filled the arrogant souls of these fashionable New England traders of human flesh! Undoubtedly, many of these slave traders might have been charter members of the church in the old South and would joyfully sing John Newton's classic congregational hymn "Amazing Grace."

O my child Nikki, just imagine yourself a playmate of Phillis's responding to the daily insults and moral degradation of growing up a slave girl and black—with no real protection against the cold winters of racism and oppression. O imagine yourself, my child, with no one to share the deep anguish of the soul with, except the God of "my *Pagan* land." Phillis Wheatley— a servant girl and a poet for Boston's marginalized poor—yearned for the fragrance of true freedom amidst the stench of conflict and revolutionary strife.

> Lo! Freedom comes. Th' prescient Muse foretold,
>   All Eyes th' accomplish'd Prophecy behold:
>   Her Port describ'd, "She moves divinely fair,
>   Olive and Laurel bind her golden Hair."
>   She, the bright Progeny of Heaven, descends,
>   And every Grace her sovereign Step attends;
>   For now kind Heaven, indulgent to our Prayer,
>   In smiling Peace resolves the Din of War.[2]

Nikki, my child, it has been said and some believe that young Phillis Wheatley, who was skilled in the literary traditions of Shakespeare, Swift, Pope, and Milton, was hurt by slavery but not defeated. The rhythmic accents of her graceful poetry ranged from science to religion. In the latter sense, Phillis Wheatley, as a black woman, relied upon God to achieve fame and education— the two things often denied women.

Listen up, my daughter. Let me tell you a true story concerning black women in this society. I'm telling you this story because I don't want you to ever feel inside that you can't achieve or become whatever you wanna be because of your gender. The story involves a high school classmate of mine. We finished high school in 1974; and everyone in our class knew that Pat was the brightest and best student academically. Pat was elected valedictorian by the faculty. Her main dream in life was to become a medical doctor—a pediatrician. But many of us doubted if Pat would ever see her dream come true. Why? Because in the mid-1970s fewer than 3 percent of medical school attendees were African American women. But Pat didn't give up her dream. And today, I'm happy to say, Pat is one of the leading pediatricians in the state of Georgia.

Nikki, did I ever tell you about the love and experience of Jesus? I know your mother used to take you to church school, and you gained some knowledge about Jesus of Nazareth through arts and crafts, but you see, my child, I want you to have the experience of Jesus, not just knowledge. Who is Jesus? Well, this question is easy for your father to answer. Jesus is the one who loves little children just like you and young Phillis in ages gone by. Jesus said to his rebellious disciples, "Let the little children come to me, and do not stop them; for it is to such as these that the kingdom of heaven belongs" (Matthew 19:14). So then, Nikki, I would have you remember how Jesus loves you—just as you are, in the tender beauty and virtue of your own blackness.

Nikki, you are something special to mom and dad. You are a gifted and marvelous human being. Indeed, you are young, gifted, and black. You see, my child, your giftedness arises not necessarily because you are a by-product of our seed; but because you're a child of God. Therefore, when you awake each morning from your pillow of sleep, and I have the occasion to look into your innocent eyes, what do I see? Well, like a rainbow of many colors, I see the face of Jesus, and written on that face the inscription "I love you!"

O daughter of Africa, the unbridled continent and the cradle of civilization, I must bring this meandering letter to a close. I still feel sorry that I have not always been there for you as a real father, when you needed another arm to lean on. I atone right now for my sin of neglect. I shall try to do better. I atone right now for my uneasiness and misgivings about what it means to be a real father and a black man in the same body. God knows, and I know that I know, a whole lot about the latter—just growing up in white America under the leaky umbrella of all the "isms."

O daughter of Africa and the Americas, I yearn to tell you many more things, but your tender frame is not yet ready. I could have told you more about the greatness that flows in your veins as a descendent of a royal tradition from kings and queens of the motherland. Certainly I could have told you more about the life and times of freedom's mighty warriors such as Frederick Douglass or Harriet Tubman. I certainly could have told you more about my personal daily struggles as a professional black man trying to survive in a hostile white world, where the gods of power and greed seem to write their own script. But here again, my daughter Nikki, that's an adult thing and you just wouldn't understand. To be sure, I could have told you more about how difficult it is to make it up the ladder of success in America without compromising one's values, one's religious beliefs, or the fire in one's soul.

As an absentee father, I have been an uncritical consumer of European ideas and thought systems for most of my formative years as a U.S. citizen. Perhaps this is the price Africans living in the Diaspora have had to pay for their meal ticket to survival. For example, some sociologists may call it the complex process of cultural adaptation over simple cultural adoption. I'm not sure. But Nikki, at the age of seven, this is an "adult thing" and perhaps you just wouldn't understand.

Nevertheless, it is still necessary for me to say these things. You know, my daughter, as I think about this whole matter of being a recovering consumer of European ideas, I suspect that the transformation of the interior of my being did not really come—but all so gradually—until I began to read Carter G. Woodson's book *Mis-Education of the Negro,* or as I begin to more fully understand the ethical implications of E. Franklin Frazier's classic work *Black Bourgeoisie.*

But the only thing I know that is important for you to understand is this. I am on the road to recovery. I'm not there yet, but I've turned the corner in the right direction by participating in the Million Man March. I'm sorry, Nikki, that I can't tell you more right now. I gotta get on the bus from the Washington Mall and make my way back home. Of course, in due time I yearn to tell you more about such wise ones as Sojourner Truth, Gwendolyn Brooks, Maya Angelou, Nikki Giovanni, Toni Morrison, Coretta Scott King, Rosa Parks—just to name a few. O daughter of the dream, they all started, tender and beloved in God's grace, just like you.

Now in the spirit of the Million Woman March—as the ancient God of history surely demanded in the divine court of equality—I know that you could be the best drum major of the new order, leading the parade! Although, you may be black by nature, you can still be proud by choice, as a sun-kissed daughter of the old country, the cradle of civilization. Nikki-Renée Bryant, your father is proud of you, and be assured, as the God of heaven and earth smiles upon you, that you're the key to America's future. So take heart. I love you!

Sincerely,

Your Dad

Lifting Up an Afrocentric Biblical Legacy

THE AFRICAN EXPERIENCE . . . IS PRESENT IN THE LITERATURE OF
MANY . . . PERIODS OF BIBLICAL HISTORY, AND IN ALMOST EVERY
TYPE OF LITERATURE. AFRICA FIGURES AS HOME AND PLACE OF
REFUGE FROM THE TIME OF ABRAHAM THROUGH THE TIME OF JESUS.
AFRICANS, FROM SLAVES TO RULERS, APPEAR AS ACTORS ON THE
STAGE OF HISTORY. AUTHORS OF MUCH OF THE BIBLICAL CONTENT
WERE NATIVE AFRICANS IN ORIGIN. AND IN THE VEINS OF HEBREW-
ISRAELITES-JUDAHITES-JEWISH PEOPLES FLOWED AFRICAN BLOOD.

—Charles B. Copher

As an outstanding scholar of Hebrew Scripture, Charles B. Copher
has pioneered the investigation of black presence in the ancient
world of culture and faith in general, and in the power of the biblical text in particular.[1] As one of the pillars of African American
scholarship, Copher has made a profound contribution to the
contemporary church, through linguistics and word studies, with
respect to how the Bible has its roots in African soil and how the
people portrayed in its pages include African people.

The logic of Afrocentric recognition in Hebrew Scriptures, in
Copher's view, is not an ideological attempt to blacken the Bible,
or to make black folk intellectually and morally superior to all
other peoples on this planet; rather, it is simply to bear witness to
the presence of blacks in the biblical materials and in the ancient
biblical world. From ethical and biblical perspectives, Copher's
work aids the general reader and layperson of the church in making a correction from "Whitey-anity" to authentic Christianity,

from what some black theologians call "snake-ology" to liberation theology. Put another way, the abiding contribution of Charles B. Copher, former academic dean and professor of Old Testament at the Interdenominational Theological Center for more than forty years, is the biblical grounding and confidence he gives to ordinary people of faith to make a paradigm shift from Eurocentrism to Afrocentrism in matters of discipleship and prophetic witness to the liberating gospel of Jesus Christ.

In *The Recovery of Black Presence,* Randall Bailey and Jacquelyn Grant argue that the concept of Afrocentrism, particularly in biblical studies, is an idea whose time has come in light of the legacies of slavery and racial injustice in America. They emphatically assert:

> Irrespective of one's ideological perspective on Afrocentrism, the central task of its proponents is the affirmation of the Black Presence and the reversal of the historic devaluation of Africa and the African world, both in academic and in non-academic circles. Out of this Afrocentric approach comes an African American perspective as the basis for understanding reality.[2]

They attempt to shed light on the critical concept of Afrocentrism and its implications for understanding the Million Man March by citing Gayraud Wilmore's typology in regard to five elements implicit in the notion itself.

> Gayraud Wilmore lists five points or components of this perspective: (1) freedom from White control and domination; (2) positive imagery of Africa as the land of origin; (3) social justice; (4) creative style and artistry; and (5) the unity

of the secular and the sacred. No longer is the European experience normative for interpreting Black reality, but the African world is elevated to a level of importance heretofore unknown to the western world.[3]

Here the authors suggest that African American Christians should use the Bible so that they begin to more clearly see their own experiences, dreams, and aspirations mirrored in Holy Scripture. Individually and corporately, I suspect that this is not a simple thing for black people to do because of our long history of suffering, economic exploitation, oppression, and the demoralization of having to endure more than four hundred years of slavery in the Western Hemisphere—a system of brutal subordination and apartheid that lasted from 1502 to 1888. It will not be easy for African American Christians to overcome the Eurocentric psychosocial icons of beauty, culture, art, and religion. For example, the images and icons of beauty or one's sense of colorism and aesthetics are deeply ingrained into the fabric of our cultural narrative. In the community of religion and culture, the traditional idiom that reveals, in part, our deep ambivalence about colorism finds expression in this saying I often heard growing up black in American society:

If you are White, you all right.
If you are Brown, stick around.
If you are Yellow, you're mellow.
But if you are Black, get back!

Well, brothers and sisters, with our modern and sophisticated theories of religion, psychology, and personality development, there is a tendency to laugh at such an idiomatic jingle as having no bearing on the way our cultural script or standards of beauty have shaped our character and moral view. To the contrary, why is it we spend millions of dollars each year on so-called beauty products such as hair relaxers, perm kits, skin tone creams, or facial lighteners? There is something about our cultural standards of beauty, for instance, that caters to the European aesthetic.

Afrocentrism calls into question, in the mundane world of consumption and competition, the conventional values by which we assess what is beautiful. What norms should African American Christians use to determine our sense of aesthetics? From the perspective of Afrocentrism, people of African descent no longer need to look to the European experience as normative for interpreting black reality.

To paraphrase Bailey and Grant, the new geopolitical situation for black folk in the world is simply this: the African world is elevated to a level of importance, while its people must determine their own destiny. By way of reflective comparison, this was the deeper message behind the Million Man March. It was a symbolic statement to a racist society that the first right of any oppressed people who want to be free is the right to define, name, claim, and celebrate their own reality and spirituality.

The March of the Spirit against Backlash

The Million Man March was an extraordinary journey of the human spirit. The Million Man March was all about ordinary people from many walks of life suddenly coming together—from the east and west, from the north and south—at a critical time in the nation's history, gathering in a special place for a day of prayer and spiritual renewal. The biblical imperative demands that all Christians of goodwill gather for communal prayers and forgiveness. No one imagined the tremendous size of the crowd or the chants of atonement uttered by Muslims and Christians, secular-ists and humanists, agnostics and nationalists, integrationists and separatists, and religionists and nonreligionists alike.

Moreover, the Million Man March was a movement of the spirit, a journey into the poetic mystery of the divine—writing its own Hollywood script and creating its own unsung actors and heroes, without external validation from the conventional power brokers of Tinsel Town. Although noted film producer Spike Lee recounted much of this cosmic event in the film *Get on the Bus,* the reality itself, fait accompli, was nothing less than a miracle.

As a movement of the spirit, this massive wave of humanity crashed the gates of the Washington Mall at a time when the tra-ditional custodians of European American power suddenly decided to take an unplanned day of vacation. As an eyewitness caught up in the rhythm of what Dr. King called the *Zeitgeist* more than thirty years earlier, this impressive wave of humanity, like chariots of fire, rolled up the banks of the Potomac River and profoundly affected the psychological landscape of a fragile democracy still reeling and railing from the deadly ashes of white backlash to the O. J. Simpson trial. Many of us, black and white together, silently lamented then—as I still do now—the tragic consequences or aftermath of the O.J. trial and its negative impact on the future of ethnic relations in America. Be that as it may, the Million Man March was a spiritual pilgrimage for me.

Theologically and biblically discerned, it was one spiritual moment in the ocean of time, wherein each participant—regard-less of social class, rank, or income—could sail his own small tug-boat and not be afraid of the big ships that customarily rule the political sea waves of power. Indeed, the big ships of hegemonic power sailed right out of town on this special day of Afrocentric atonement, thereby abandoning, symbolically, the seats of power in the U.S. Congress and White House—if only for twenty-four hours of uninterrupted grace and regeneration.

For African Americans, this is one of the joys and moral by-products of the journey of the Spirit. What I am trying to suggest about spiritual pilgrimage is simply this: as men of power plot, God plans a way of deliverance. As with the Old Testament story of Joseph, whose brothers threw him into a pit and left him for dead, we might say that "they meant it for evil but God meant it for good."

Thus the whole notion of the Million Man March as a journey of the Spirit gives us a profound clue into God's divine arithmetic. While others plot against the forces of goodwill and black communal renewal, God plans a highway to journey through a "valley of dry bones" to the halls of Congress to make a case for an alternative vision of America. This vision is rooted not in the Jeffersonian paradigm of democracy, which allowed for the moral compromise of conscience by the southern white plantation owners on the question of holding slaves as property or economic capital, but rather in the liberationist paradigm of Harriet Tubman and Frederick Douglass. Spiritually and politically, these champions of freedom possessed an uncommon faith concerning the truth of moral struggle, namely, "one man or woman with God is a majority!"

Uses of the Bible in Black Life

There are many critical questions on the front burner of one's consciousness that relate to the Bible and the African American experience.[4] The Bible itself is a dialogical book in nature because so many people—from divergent social backgrounds, ethnicities, classes, nationalities, religious hierarchies, and gender or lifestyle orientation—gather to read and study the Holy Scriptures. For some, the Bible is the redemptive story of God's liberating activity in Jesus Christ.[5] For others, the Bible is simply the living Word of God for the people of God. The Bible is not a philosophical treatise on the nature of truth, but rather the Bible is the truth about God's self-disclosure to sinful and broken humanity. But the real questions that ring through my own mind as a participant in the Million Man March are, namely, What is the use or authority of the Bible for the black moral life? In light of the March, what has the Bible to do with black suffering and rage in America? Put another way, we may simply ponder or ask, What, then, is the use of the Bible?

Here I wish to propose a thin sketch or an Afrocentric ethical perspective, which may include these functional elements in black life:

1. *The Bible is a praise book.* In the life and faith of the church, the Bible has been prominently used as a source of human praise to the Divine. From a black religio-historical perspective, theologians and sociologists such as C. Eric Lincoln and E. Franklin Frazier have pointed out that the black church, as a social center of community life in the antebellum South, was originally organized as a house of praise. For example, the black church as an social institution in America began in 1773 in Silver Bluffs, South Carolina, not as a house of paupers, but as the soulful house of praise. For example, slaves were oriented to a soulful pattern of black worship down by the creek, away from the big house, where they could tell God all about their troubles! They envisioned the Bible as the normative source book of divine praise and adoration to the Triune God, who is worthy to be praised. The psalmist echoes, "Make a joyful noise to the Lord, all the earth. Worship the Lord with gladness; come into his presence with singing" (Psalm 100:1–2).

2. *The Bible is a wisdom book.* The question of wisdom is the question of ethical perspective in the moral life of African

Americans. In a manner of speaking, perspective on the use of the Bible is critically tied in with our understanding of who God is or whether God cares about the dual situation of racism and sexism in church and society. As a source book of wisdom, the believer may be prone to ponder further, for instance, the questions: Does God hear and answer the prayer of the marginalized and hurting ones in our world? On what moral grounds can one speak of the presence of God in the Million Man March? Were the organizers of the Million Man March inherently sexist or anti-womanist and anti-feminist in their strategic exclusion of the daughters, mothers, and grandmothers of the liberation struggle for black empowerment in our fragile global village? Indeed, the voices of wisdom, implicitly and explicitly revealed through the biblical materials, would have us ponder these ethical questions of conscience, faith, and atonement. In short, we are reminded that "the beginning of wisdom is this: Get wisdom, and whatever else you get, get insight. Prize her highly, and she will exalt you; she will honor you if you embrace her" (Proverbs 4:7–8).

3. *The Bible is an inclusive book.* Metaphorically considered, the Bible is useful in the moral life of faith and struggle for "drawing circles" rather than "building walls." Here I think that the critical dialectic of faith and reason may serve to illustrate the point of biblical inclusivity. As Reinhold Niebuhr, a renowned teacher of applied Christianity and social theory, often pointed out, reason is morally good as an instrument of communication and enlightenment; but it can also become a selfish servant of the will—especially the will to power. Now in the latter sense, rationalists sometimes draw a circle and cut marginalized people out, but faith activists build bridges of compassion and justice, and then invite the rejected and marginalized people to "come on over the wall" and join the new community of God, without regard to gender,

class, color, nationality, or religious persuasion. As it is affirmed in Holy Scriptures, "There is no longer Jew or Greek, there is no longer slave or free, there is no longer male or female; for you are all one in Christ Jesus" (Galatians 3:28).

4. *The Bible is a liberation book.* For people with a shared memory of suffering and oppression, the Bible is a book of hope and promise. What is hoped for by the oppressed is authentic freedom. What is promised as witnessed in the God of the Bible is deliverance. Therefore, for the sons and daughters of the Million Man March and its vicarious supporters throughout the world where suffering and injustice are daily endured, the cry for liberation is not a game, but a gift of God's liberating activity in history. The Bible is the universal testimony to God's liberating activity in Jesus Christ. In the final analysis, I want to strongly affirm that the Bible is a book about us—a covenant and pilgrim people of the Way, who know the meaning of exile and the promise of deliverance. The Bible is a book of life-giving stories about God's relationship to us, to creation, and to the church of Jesus Christ in the world. The Bible has authority for the moral life and for Christian witness to the power of the gospel only because we believe and accept the stories of biblical faith as our stories.[6]

For the morally sensitive believer, it is the power of the gospel that expresses the important place and use of the Bible in human community. The Bible has moral authority to the extent that its adherents believe and affirm the essential claims of the biblical narrative itself. As a life-giving book, the Bible is not primarily a chronicle concerning ancient history, philosophy, archaeology, or some fossilized period from the distant past. Rather, the Bible is the community of faith's storybook, which can be summed up in one word, *liberation.*

In retrospect, it seems to me that the major organizers behind the Million Man March, the quiet social engineers and the foot soldiers who kept the large crowd of people orderly and peaceful, affirmed the vision of liberation. Whether one uses the language of atonement or of moral struggle, the real glue that holds the center of black hope together is the vision of liberation—regardless of one's particular religion, class, rank, or social stratum in society. For those courageous participants on October 16, 1995, the passion behind the Million Man March reflects a deep truth because of one reason and only one reason: a unifying vision for genuine liberation. Nothing less will satisfy the hunger of a people who have engaged in a protracted struggle against the sins of slavery, Jim Crowism, bigotry, police brutality, black apathy, the agonizing pain of second-class citizenship, and the proverbial "glass ceiling" of corporate America.

Theologically, I think that James H. Evans's book *We Have Been Believers* may illustrate nicely the deeper vision behind the Million Man March, especially from ethical and historical perspectives.

> The vision of a new order was indispensable to Africans languishing in the foul embrace of slavery because it kept the fires of freedom burning in their hearts. Yet they were not content to claim solely an inner freedom. The idea of the reign of God on the Promised Land compelled them to proclaim and approximate it in their individual and collective existence.[7]

The deeper issues of the Million Man March were not about controversial leaders versus safe leaders of the civil rights movement who differ over doctrinal belief systems that separate Christians from Muslims and Protestants from Catholics or Jews, but rather the perennial problems and core issues revolving around the dialectic of suffering and hope.

The apostle Paul envisioned well this perennial dialectic amidst the paradox of human existence when he said, "We are afflicted in every way, but not crushed; perplexed, but not driven to despair; persecuted, but not forsaken; struck down, but not destroyed" (2 Corinthians 4:8–9). Thus, the legacy of the March may center its lasting contributions more in how we appropriate the wider vision and on how we engage in the art of critical thinking about thinking than in any particular government-based policy or community-based program itself. The legacy is also one that provides a new forum for conversation, dialogue, and cooperative economics between black Muslims and their Christian brothers and sisters. To this end, I wish to propose the following credo as an initial step toward genuine dialogue and communal conversation in light of critical concerns and issues in the black moral life.

Toward a Common Credo for Muslims and Christians

1. I believe and affirm that people universally share a common humanity. Therefore, the challenge for Christian morality and Muslim morality is to bring every phase of our common behavior under the judgment of a merciful God.

2. I believe and affirm that children and adults alike have a need and a universal yearning for the Divine, in order to atone for wrongdoing and the sins that so easily beset us.

3. I believe and affirm that all people on the planet—regardless of race, creed, color, class, ethnicity, religious doctrine, disability, or sexual orientation—are brothers and sisters caught in life's tedious journey and tied into an inescapable network of vulnerability and mutuality.

4. I believe that we are saved not by fancy theologies, by stringent dogmatic creeds, or by worshiping at the altar of moralism and legalism, but rather by God's grace "through faith, and even that is a gift of God."

5. I believe that one of the ironies of history in our time is that the white man is too concerned about the power he might lose, and the black man is too angry about the power he had and lost since the crafting of the glorious Egyptian pyramids—so that neither can think clearly about the future.

6. Hence, I believe that the essential unity we seek or the "super-bowl" of our common humanity is cracked and marred by racial division and fear arising from Anglophobia and Afrophobia.

7. I believe and affirm, as a confessing Christian in Jesus Christ, that a new humanity and fellowship are made possible through loving acts of forgiveness and grace.

8. I believe and affirm that we must move from a pathology of immoral power, which capitalism breeds, to a psychology of loving power that enables us to transform structures of cruelty in the wilderness of white America into communities of kindness.

9. I believe and affirm that the black churches and Muslim mosques in America still offer the best hope for the future of our children—despite the failures peculiar to all human institutions.

10. I believe and affirm, in the words of a famous African proverb, that "it takes a village to raise a child." Therefore, let us not abandon our babies and children to the evil forces in society.

Open Letter from Brotha to Brotha

LIFE IS A SHORT WALK. THERE IS SO LITTLE TIME AND SO MUCH LIVING TO ACHIEVE.

—John Oliver Killens

I have only just a minute,
Only sixty seconds in it,
Forced upon me—can't refuse it,
Didn't seek it, didn't choose it.
But it's up to me to use it.

—Benjamin E. Mays

Dear Soul Brotha,

I am writing this letter to you because I strongly believe that it is time for us to stop playing games. It's time to start taking care of business again. You know, once upon a time we used to joyfully greet one another with the black handshake and a bear hug, but nowadays we seem not to greet one another at all, but rather bear an envious grudge.

Once upon a time, we turned to each other in time of need, but nowadays we turn on each other because of greed!

Once upon a time, one could see the children of the community dancing in the streets to the rhythms of *Soul Train,* carefree and without groaning, but nowadays there is grief-stricken mourning. Careful observation would suggest that far too many black folks are mourning in the streets to the lamenting raindrops of mothers' tears, gushing from their eyes like the mighty streams from Africa's Victoria Falls as a result of too many senseless killings of innocent children in the neighborhood. And what about the tendency on the part of some of us to wanna beat up on black women. I ask you, should we be loving our women or beating them up?

Listen up, Brotha-man. I wanna tell you a true story about the silliness and wrongfulness of beating up on the sisters. As a young boy growing up in the deep South, I often would observe older black males talking about their romantic pursuits. I overheard, once upon a time, one brotha say to another, "Man, if you beat your old lady, she'll love you more. You can't be all nice to no woman; my woman likes me to treat her rough and hard. That will make her crazy about me!"

Brotha-man, that kind of thing about African American women really tripped me out. I was puzzled and confused about male–female relationships at that time, especially in regard to how I was supposed to treat the opposite sex on a date, for instance. But looking back on those formative teenage years, I can truly say that the only thing that saved me from the madness of female bashing was observing my father's behavior toward my mother. And the testimony is this. I never saw my father hit my mother. So then I don't hit or abuse my wife or daughter. I think the bottom line to this beating thing is a very simple, yet awesome, lesson: We live what we learn!

In the prophetic lyrics of Marvin Gaye, we cry out from the pit of our souls, "What's going on?" Brotha-man, what's happening to black America? Why are there so many young mothers crying? Why are there so many of us dying? Why are there, seemingly, more funerals on a weekly basis than joyful celebrations in the inner-city neighborhoods? Living at the intersection of rage and despair, many of us are still prone to agree with Marvin Gaye's social analysis that "far too many are crying . . . and far too many are dying."

Brotha-man, I can remember once upon a time when we used to see self-styled visionaries amid the street corner societies of Harlem, Roxbury, Chicago's South Side, or South Central Los Angeles preaching the gospel of black pride. You see brotha, I remember when these self-styled visionaries would be most sincere in their passion and fervor about building up the community. Indeed, these African American visionaries would often shout to an attentive crowd:

> "Hey, brothers and sisters, what time is it? Do you hear me today? I said, what time is it?" And suddenly, like a rushing mighty wind, a participant-spectator from the pumped-up crowd would echo, "It's revolution time! It's nation-building time! It is time to make a change! It is time for all the brothers and beautiful black sisters, saints and sinners living in white America, to take care of business!"

Brotha-man, now I ask you, was this rhetoric simply idle talk, an idealistic expression of unbridled egoism locked up in the souls of black folk? Was it merely a form of repressed rage that had, by the laws of human nature, to find psychological relief? Or was it a hunger so deep that only the taste of true freedom was fully satisfying? You make the call; you call the shots; you exercise the privilege of moral examination. The ball is in your court. You make the choice, as moral agent.

For example, you hold the ball, like Michael Jordan of the Chicago Bulls, for the last crucial shot of the game. But this time, the outcome is not two more points or even another game won.

The choices facing the African American community are literally life-and-death choices. Perhaps the best word to describe our current situation is *genocide*.

The African American community now faces a crisis of enormous proportion. We are literally on the edge of self-destruction without the reinvigoration of the spirit of the Million Man March. Indeed, it is the duty of African American men to step up to the free-throw line and at least sink a foul shot that will forge a culture of resistance to the despair, hopelessness, and nihilism all around us—written in bold ink on the faces of the community's children and marginalized poor.

The crisis in our community today is to save our children, set free the oppressed, and empower from the bottom up. Brotha-man, if we fail in doing these things, I am afraid that the word *genocide* will seal our fate in American society. Enslaved by the cruel chains of unfortunate events of history, moral and political speech will not give us the courage to step up to the free-throw line to take care of business! Here I shall state the matter in poetic form:

Brotha-man, I call you
    Tomorrow may be too late,
    Unless we return "Black Pearls"
    Sad, sad will be our fate.

    Brotha-man, I call you
    from hypocrisy, drugs, and drifting
    To do the right thing;
    But the way most Black folk
    Live today is a crying
    Shame.

Brotha-man, I call you today
from the despair of resignation,
like sounds of ghetto madness
Deep in the night—to the
Hope of revolution and salvation.

Brotha-man, I call you today
like an African warrior,
Standing strong and tall;
For if we, once again,
Embrace the principle of unity,
Our community will not fall.

For black men in North American society, the notion of step-ping up to the line to take care of business is an idea whose time has come. Living on the rugged edges of these perilous times, there have been many men of color who challenged us to struggle with the nightmare of American racism and black rage. Brotha-man, do you see where I'm coming from? By that I mean that the Zulu call to take care of business may take many forms depend-ing on one's ideology, philosophy, religious orientation, moral per-suasion, experiences, and social context. You see, my brotha, part of the perennial historical problem of black suffering arises from the fact that African Americans live in a peculiar, confusing, and strange culture that makes it difficult for the individual to decide—ideologically—what is the good and right thing to do.

Indeed, the use of the metaphor "step up to the line" means many things to different people. For example, the events and forces shaping the drama of black suffering in America connect us—ideologically and spiritually—with many forms of black nationalism in the persons of Martin R. Delaney, Marcus Garvey, and Malcolm X, on the one hand; and the intellectual architects of the philosophy of integration-assimilation, on the other.

Brotha-man, as I see it, these prophetic warriors of authentic freedom, in the form of radical integrationism, would include such moral leaders and teachers as Frederick Douglass, Mary McLeod Bethune, and Rosa Parks, to name only a few. Again, I plead with you to recognize and understand that the perennial problem we face, in light of the spirit of the Million Man March, is not the simple proposition in contemporary society to step up to the line, but rather to find which line. I submit that the question itself challenges our deepest moral assumptions about the meaning of black life in America, that is to say, our bedrock values concerning the quest for identity, purpose, consciousness of God, and a vision beyond the mountain of white racism.

Brotha-man, it seems to me that I somehow vaguely remember from my first history lesson on my father's front porch, in the deep South, where he talked to me about W. E. B. DuBois's book *The Souls of Black Folk*. With a profound sense of duty and moral rage, Big Brother DuBois stepped up to the line and slam-dunked in his keen awareness and articulation that the "problem of the twentieth century is the problem of the color line."[1]

Brotha-man, as I write this letter to you, I am compelled to ponder and to agonize over what Big Brother DuBois would possibly say to us black men who gathered in the nation's capitol on October 16, 1995, in light of what he said nearly one hundred years ago, when these prophetic words in regard to the color line were first uttered. I also pray you to ponder the passion and mystery of this one solitary sentence: "The problem of the twentieth century is the problem of the color line."

Significant images and ironies must have been engendered in 1903, when Big Brother DuBois penned this famous sentence of

American literature. Did he not venture to reveal to us something deeper than his own solitary soul? Did he not dare to reveal to us something deeper than the wellspring of his own creative intellect and brilliant mind? Did he not dare to sketch the banks of a deep black river that still surges inside each of us now while pondering the multidimensional problems of color and class, gender and lifestyle orientation, power and privilege, and the meaning of religion and rap culture in American society? What hard lessons of history would Big Brother DuBois have us remember? To be sure, these are some of the questions and concerns I carry inside of me during our struggle with what it means to step up to the line and take care of business in the aftermath of the Million Man March.

Brotha-man, I must admit in this letter to you that I hear and understand that a lot of stuff went down concerning the money collected at the Million Man March itself. For example, how much was actually raised in the open collection, which the ushers passed the bucket through the massive crowd? Where did the money go? What did it pay for? Who really got some? I remember putting some money in the bucket myself, but what purpose did it serve? For the critical and inquiring mind, some of us, Brotha-man, just might remember the key line from a popular movie: "Show me the money!" Well, I'm not so much concerned about the money from the Million Man March, except that it is symbolic, in our collective consciousness, of the imperative call to accountability and self-responsibility as human beings on this planet.

Brotha-man, all the big fuss and talk in the aftermath of the Million Man March may be nothing more than blowing hot air unless we take responsibility for our own families, children, schools, and community social institutions. Therefore, I feel and believe, Brotha-man, that we must even take responsibility for the way we talk to one another, you know, the funny and not so funny words we use in casual conversation.

For example, I wish to illustrate this point by sharing with you, Brotha-man, a recent story about a black Muslim and a black Christian. These two men were in strong dialogue and heated conversation about the issue of welfare and why so many young black teen mothers are, seemingly, so dependent upon the federal government for handouts. Now in the heat of social dialogue, the black Christian lost his cool and called the black Muslim a "nigger." After a long pause in speech on the part of the Muslim brother, he quietly retorted, "Listen up, man. We need to end right now this conversation about our young sister who is a teen mother on welfare. I don't even wanna. So there you go with the n-word. After all, why would one black one call another black man nigger? Listen up, brother. Think about it. Is that a true sign of self-knowledge? Why get angry and use the same word to react or greet me that the white man did for four hundred years to degrade and humiliate black folk? *Must we be niggers forever?*"

Well, now you see, my brotha, this story—which happens all the time in the marketplace of black culture—illustrates that we who live in America and are black still have a problem internally and psychologically with this word *nigger*. I wonder, why do we use it so much? In the sociopolitical terrain of black culture, God did not create people of African descent to refer to each other as "niggers." Why, brothers, do we do that to ourselves? The burden of the ethical demands that we face the linguistic beast inside of us and resist the impulse and attitude to utter—either in times of black-on-black rage or in friendly conversation—the inflammatory word "nigger"!

Brotha-man, I realize that this letter has been too long in the making. I realize that we've got many problems to ponder and solve before we can sleep easily tonight—and this stuff about "nigger this, nigger that" is just one of many hair-raising problems that we face in society. So then, genetically speaking, I know and affirm that we were not born "niggers" but human beings with a natural inclination toward achievement, enlightenment, community-building, and a passion for the Divine. In this tedious journey we call life, I submit, brotha-man, that we ain't there yet. But I believe that spiritually we're on the path. So, as I close this letter, I say, "Take courage." Therefore, I give to you the words my father gave to me and that I will give to my sons in the aftermath of the Million Man March regarding the virtue of courage: "The virtue of courage is the virtue to be cool. The ethic of coolness is the bedrock value system of how Black men relate to each other and bond together as people of faith and social struggle."

Brotha-man, you know what? A survey in *Ebony* magazine regarding the ten most important qualities that black women admire in black men revealed that the number-one quality black women admire is the element of coolness in their menfolk. The ethic of coolness will, therefore, keep us out of deep trouble and on the right track.

In short, Brotha-man, we must have the courage to be cool under the extraordinary circumstances of institutionalized oppression, suffering, and degradation in America. In the final analysis of our conversation, I suspect, Brotha-man, that the ethic of coolness is an eternal glow in the human heart to keep us smart; the ethic of coolness is the right step to enhance our pep; and it is deep in places of the soul to make us whole.

Well, Brotha-man, it is time for me to close this letter. There is always much more to be said than we seem to have time to listen. I'm not sure if anybody in America really wants to listen anymore to what black men are saying and feeling. If nobody cares about us, shouldn't we care about us? If nobody cares about the black man's spirituality, for instance, shouldn't we care? Should we not ponder the boundaries of our own nurture and centeredness if we are to step up to the line and take care of business?

Sincerely,

Your Soul Brotha

Recovering Hope from Martin and Malcolm

THERE IS NO FEAR IN LOVE; BUT PERFECT LOVE CASTS OUT FEAR.

—1 John 4:18

Hope is like the sun, which,
As we journey toward it,
Casts the shadow of our
Burden behind us.

—S. Smiles

Two of the most compelling and influential personalities of the twentieth century—in religion and in the human rights movement around the world—are Martin Luther King Jr. and Malcolm X. The perennial struggle on the part of ethically sensitive persons to understand the legacy of the Million Man March is rooted in the radically different and conflicted visions of black life in white America. I hold the moral point of view that one cannot possibly understand or grasp the historical significance of the Million Man March in isolation from the philosophy and critical thoughts of Martin and Malcolm. Philosophically and religiously considered, they represent both the creative tensions and the ideological divisions of the Million Man March, in terms of attitudes, values, and beliefs in symbolic expressions of black unity and human dignity.

Malcolm's Social Development

There is no personality more colorful, no political activist more controversial, and no black leader more ideologically revered and socially feared than the man we call Malcolm X. Formally, some writers and scholars refer to him as El Hajj Malik El Shabazz, signifying a new name and a new self-understanding. Malcolm X, the Muslim minister and social activist, was born in Omaha, Nebraska, on May 19, 1925, four years before Martin Luther King Jr. He was the seventh of thirteen children in the family of Earl and Louise Little.

A proud and intelligent man, Earl Little was a traveling Baptist preacher whose work and moral philosophy were inspired by and connected with Marcus Garvey's United Negro Improvement Association. Little's activist approach to the black condition of suffering and oppression in America placed him in danger from white hate groups, but dealing with this was nothing new for him. Three of his brothers had been killed by white men, and he himself had already lost an eye in violent confrontations.

Malcolm X later reflected on the pervasiveness of black suffering in America by saying: "We didn't land on Plymouth Rock, Plymouth Rock landed on us!" While reflecting on the current topic, a flood of questions rush to our minds: Why must we remember Malcolm X? Why did so many Americans see him as a threat to the social system? Did America see Malcolm simply as an angry black man from the streets of the ghetto who ran numbers and hustled women? Was he the embodiment of the media's evil, radical revolutionary bent on violence and tearing down America? Was there common ground between Malcolm and Martin on the tough questions of identity and black progress? Why can we not easily dismiss the lives and memories of both Malcolm and Martin from the landscape of American social conscience? What can we learn about ourselves from Malcolm and Martin in light of the Million Man March?

Three current assumptions or moral convictions seem appropriate to me. First, we as educators and students tend to know more about the life and thoughts of Martin Luther King Jr. than Malcolm X because of the peculiar leadership configuration of the civil rights movement in the 1960s. Second, I hold the conviction that Malcolm X, unlike Martin Luther King Jr., was a neglected and ideologically disvalued leader of the 1960s, partly because he was greatly feared by the dominant culture and often misunderstood by black people themselves. Third, a resurgence of interest in Malcolm X is occurring among many blacks and other segments of the society. This phenomenon is due in part, I suspect, to recent movies such as Spike Lee's *Malcolm X* and the increase of racism and ethnic violence in our culture.

For example, I teach a course at Webster University on issues related to Malcolm X and Martin Luther King Jr. During the orientation session I ask, "What is your earliest memory of Malcolm or Martin?" The overwhelming response often goes like this. White students say, "My parents taught me that Malcolm X was a hatemonger and black militant who pulled society down by stirring up racial strife." Some black students tended to respond, "Malcolm X was evil, Martin King was real good, so stay away from those sneaky black Muslims!" The impressions that Malcolm and Martin have left behind run the gamut from prophetic hero in search of an integrated, just society to the "Rambo" villain, bent on destroying all "blue-eyed devils" and the social institutions in our American democratic republic.

Like many of his contemporaries, Malcolm discovered that growing up black in America wasn't easy. His early childhood showed the strains of both poverty and prejudice. His family moved from Omaha to Milwaukee, Wisconsin, then to Lansing, Michigan, where they bought a house in the white section of town. This immediately created a problem with the Black Legion, a local white terrorist group. When Malcolm was four, two white men burned their house to the ground, but no one was injured. When he was six, his father was killed, reportedly in a trolley car accident, but the incident was commonly understood to have been a racially motivated murder. His mother held the family together for a number of years, until a promising relationship with a man ended and she suffered a complete breakdown. For the rest of her life she was confined to a state mental hospital in Michigan.

All the children in the family except the two oldest were sent to foster homes. Malcolm was thirteen and was placed in the home of a local black family, the Gohannas. He was rebellious and was later expelled from school, which led to his transfer to a detention home run by the Swerlins, a white couple. They grew to like him "as a mascot" and placed him in Mason Junior High School, where he was accepted in a similar way. In the second semester of the seventh grade he was elected president of his class, but despite his popularity the students thought nothing of telling "nigger jokes" in his presence.

That summer, when he was fourteen, his oldest sister, Ella, brought him for a visit to her home in Boston. He appreciated her comfortable life amid many other black people and decided that was for him. The eighth grade back in Mason went well until one of his favorite teachers, from whom he had earned very high grades, responded one day to his statement that he wanted to become a lawyer: "A lawyer? That's no realistic goal for a nigger. Why don't you plan on carpentry?" From that point on Malcolm began to distrust whites and withdrew from them. The change was noticeable and officials decided to move him to another family. He wanted to move to Boston and live with his sister, and the arrangements were made for that move immediately upon his completion of eighth grade.

In Boston, despite his sister's best efforts, he soon fell in with a crowd of streetwise hustlers and gained a hard city edge. He held a number of jobs and sold marijuana cigarettes on the side. He never got beyond a formal ninth-grade education, though he later educated himself. He found a job selling sandwiches on the New Haven railroad line running between Boston and New York, which introduced him to the New York nightlife, which made Boston pale by comparison.

In his autobiography, Malcolm X recalled the nature of his hustler and happy-go-lucky lifestyle imitating white standards and white values of beauty in hairstyle:

> I vowed that I'd never again be without a conk, and I never was for many years. This was my first really big step toward self-degradation: when I endured all of that pain, literally burning my flesh to have it look like a white man's hair. (I had joined that multitude of Negro men and women in America who are brainwashed into believing that the black people are "inferior"—and white people "superior"—that they will even violate and mutilate their God-created bodies to try to look "pretty" by white standards.)[1]

Martin's Social Development

Martin Luther King Jr.'s social world was culturally different from the concrete urban jungle of the underclass that Malcolm knew firsthand in cities such as Boston, New York, and Detroit. Martin enjoyed family solidarity, education, emotional wellness, and a strong faith in the triune God in a middle-class home environment. Born into a family of Baptist preachers and educators, the young M.L., as he was affectionately called, became a progressive advocate for freedom and justice.

According to Robert Franklin, when King was young, his parents noticed M.L.'s unusual ability to endure pain. Although in obvious pain during spankings, he refused to cry. But his defenses were not quite prepared for the injury that white America would soon inflict. In his biography *Let the Trumpet Sound,* Stephen B. Oates reports King's preschool years, when his closest playmate was a white boy whose father owned the store across the street from the King home.[2] When the two friends entered school in 1935, they attended separate schools. One day the parents of his friend announced that M.L. could no longer play with their son. Their explanation was, "Because we are white and you are colored." Later, around the dinner table, his parents responded to his hurt by telling him the story of the black experience in America. Historically, through such conversations as this, black youth have been socialized into the protest tradition of the black community and church.

Martin's mother sought to soothe his wounded ego and to reinforce his self-esteem by telling him, "You must never feel that you are less than anybody else. You must always feel that you are somebody."

The Pain of Black Exclusion

White liberals and the dominant media—whenever they follow the story of Martin, Malcolm, and the 1960s—usually raise one issue: Do black people in America want integration or separation? For a people with a shared memory of suffering and oppression, the question itself is false and misleading. The usual inquiries assume that oppressed blacks of early 1960s somehow had real power to magically change the normative structures of the American sociopolitical system by shouting, "Black power!"

Preston N. Williams in "The Ethics of Black Power," an article describing the ethical aspects of the black church–black theology phenomenon, suggests that black power as a concept came about as a result of our exclusion from equal participation in the mainstream of American life. Our separation and marginalization constitute a profound ethical dilemma in the body politic of the wider Christian community.

> The black church/black theology movement exists because of the past, present, and continuing desire of white Christians to deny that the black man is a child of God. Ninety percent of black Christians are outside the white church not because of their lack of a coherent theological system but simply because they are black. . . . The first ethical aspect of the black church phenomenon then is its willingness to make plain the actual state of relationships among white and black Christians. We are separated brethren. No amount of special departments—social justice or church and race—no number of national and international conferences on race presided over by white Americans of distinction; no enumeration of white persons who have given their life in service to the Negro; no counting of the good deeds performed by . . . white Christians can obscure this fact.[3]

Thus, our very blackness or separateness constitutes, deep down, a more subtle moral link in our understanding of the philosophy and theology of both Malcolm X and Martin Luther King Jr. Put another way, Malcolm and Martin knew what it meant to be black. And they knew what it meant to feel the pain of exclusion in white America. Therefore, Martin and Malcolm embraced and advocated their own ethical brand of black power as a viable strategy of social uplifting and community revitalization. That is, both leaders were apostles of hope.

Some have said and more believe that many philosophers, theologians, preachers, and prophets of African descent have cried out for black power. Indeed, black abolitionists such as Martin R. Delany, Frederick Douglass, Harriet Tubman, Sojourner Truth, and Phillis Wheatley raised their voices in militant protest against white racism and the dehumanizing system of slavery. Malcolm and Martin were no different. As prophetic voices and social activists, they were intellectual and spiritual children of the historical legacy of black self-determination.

In reflecting on Martin and Malcolm, however, one needs to differentiate between the ideological split of integrationists and separatists on the one hand, and liberationists and ethno-relative humanists on the other. The old view of race, framed as the so-called integrationist-separatist dilemma, is a false interpretative scheme for understanding the complex value systems and methodological orientations of Martin and Malcolm—false because the conceptual and ideological dichotomy is too sharp. Such a social analysis gives the impression to ordinary American citizens— black and white—that these men were staunch enemies and social adversaries.

Martin and Malcolm may not have been on the same page, but they certainly were reading from the same book. That is, they were reacting to the same texts of American cultural imperialism. They were beaten by the same context of black suffering at the hands of white racism. They were treated to the same story of black rage as a result of psychological brainwashing and the systemic assault and dismantling of language, culture, and religion by whites for more than four hundred years. They were assaulted by the same subtext of segregation on the American soil which unwittingly promoted and sanctioned racial bigotry and the supremacist attitudes of whites over blacks.

During the civil rights movement in the 1960s, both Martin and Malcolm spoke out clearly. One unofficial slogan was "Negroes, last hired, first fired." Their language as spokespersons for social justice reflected Hillel's famous phrases relating to the plight of marginalized European Jews: "If I am not for myself, who will be for me? [But] if I am only for myself, what am I? And, if not now, when?"[4]

Both Malcolm and Martin had keen intellects in discerning and articulating the profound moral contradictions of American democracy when it came to the plight of blacks and other people of color. They both believed in the philosophy of black pride and self-esteem. They both advocated self-acceptance as a form of empowerment. With the wisdom of African princes and sages, they carefully avoided the pitfall of "divide and conquer" so pervasive in the dominant culture when dealing with controversial patterns of national black leadership in America.

Malcolm and Martin were on different pages—in terms of theoretical approaches, religion, and lifestyles—but in the same book when it came to understanding what it means to grow up black in America. Whether one is a hustling pimp on the streets of Harlem or a recipient of a Ph.D. in systematic theology from Boston University, in the eyes of the white oppressor you're still a "nigger"! Ethnic relations in our social world have not changed significantly since then. Unfortunately, for many upwardly mobile professionals in academic institutions or corporate America, the perception of the black person, despite middle-class status, is this: "Just another nigger with a Ph.D., Mercedes, BMW, living in the suburbs!" or "Just another nigger down in the ghetto hustling drugs and money, killing off one another!"

For Malcolm the American dilemma is not purely a black thing or a white thing, but the agonizing dialectic of the human condition. When Malcolm returned to the United States on November 24, 1964, after spending a total of twenty-five weeks abroad, he delivered the so-called Audubon Speeches. Shortly before his death, he spoke about black problems and the need for human liberation in a global context.

> Brothers and sisters, it's not a case of worrying about what's going on in Africa before we get things straight over here. It's a case of realizing that the Afro-American problem is not a Negro problem, or an American problem, but a human problem, a problem for humanity. When you realize that, when you look at your and my problem in the context of the entire world and see that it is a world problem, . . . then you and I become allies and we can put forth our efforts in a way to get the best results.[5]

Even though Malcolm clearly advocated black cultural nationalism as the road to manhood or self-realization, and even though Martin emphasized an integrationist love monism as the right methodological road map, they both shared the ultimate goal of liberation as human beings struggling to find meaning amidst the problems, ambiguities, and social contradictions of historical existence.

Key Moral Principles

What sort of moral principles undergirded Malcolm and Martin's vision of blacks in American society? What shape or form should the moral struggle for freedom and human dignity take? For Malcolm, the moral struggle was a direct philosophical outgrowth of the teachings of Marcus Garvey, who said, "Up, you mighty race, you can accomplish what you will!"[6] One of the perennial burdens of the black man, as Malcolm X saw it, was the burden of black people being brainwashed by whites in this society for more than 350 years.

Now because of this oppressive pattern in American history, the black man's mind had to be Africanized and "de-niggered." Five moral principles undergirded Garveyism: race pride, self-respect, African nationalism, separatism, and self-determination. First, race pride is a normative source for people of color and those victimized by racial bigotry and exclusion. Similar to Martin Luther King Jr. in this regard, Malcolm X believed that blacks must take pride in their own culture and African heritage. Here he emphatically recalls how his father took pride in being a black man, not a Negro:

> I can remember hearing of "Adam driven out of the garden into the caves of Europe," "Africa for the Africans," "Ethiopians, Awake!" And my father would talk about how it would not be much longer before Africa would be completely run by Negroes—"by black men," was the phrase he always used. "No one knows when the hour of Africa's redemption cometh. It is in the wind. It is coming. One day, like a storm, it will be here."[7]

Second, self-respect made no sense to Malcolm unless one was willing to take responsibility for one's own actions. For example, during his days of hustling on the streets of the ghetto dealing with drugs, crime, and abuse, Malcolm had little occasion to call for a cultural revolution or to express artistic creativity. He felt that before these positive things of black culture can occur, self-respect must be in place.

Third, the dynamic principle of African nationalism was close to the heartbeat of El Hajj Malik el Shabazz, as he felt then that approximately 22 million black brothers and sisters had been denied a sense of a homeland—both spiritually and culturally. Concerning the recovery of cultural roots and Pan-African sentiments, he wrote:

> And I believe . . . that if we migrated back to Africa culturally, philosophically and psychologically, while remaining here physically, the spiritual bond that would develop between us and Africa through this cultural . . . and psychological migration . . . would enhance our position here, because we would have our contacts with them acting as roots or foundations behind us. You never will have a foundation in America.[8]

Fourth, the principle of separatism according to Malcolm is interesting as well as problematic. Ideologically, it is the point where the moral contrast between Malcolm and Martin is most clearly divided regarding the future struggles of people of African descent for genuine freedom and human fulfillment. For Malcolm the idea of choosing between integrationism and separatism was not the issue. The real issue, he reminded us, was one of being recognized and respected as a free human being. Was that asking for too much?

Fifth is the principle of self-determination—dynamic in its nature and expressive of the maturing social vision of Malcolm X, especially in terms of global awareness. For example, following his travels to Mecca, Africa, and Europe, Malcolm experienced a paradigm shift from a separatist vision to a more universal and inclusive vision of humanity. It is precisely here, at this point, where the previously diverging moral perspectives of Malcolm and Martin come together. They engage us at a deeper level: a level deeper than skin, deeper than social class, and deeper than gender or religious ideology. What is envisioned is the oneness of the structure of humanity itself. Martin emphatically asserts, "It really boils down to this: that all life is interrelated. We are caught in an inescapable network of mutuality tied into a single garment of destiny. Whatever affects one directly affects all indirectly. We are made to live together because of the interrelated structure of reality."[9]

What we have in King is not a dreamer, but rather a genuine theologian of social action who challenged America to face up to its complex social problems. For instance, in King's own social analysis of American society he identified a threefold socioeconomic problem that entails issues associated with poverty, prejudice, and ignorance.

As a theologian of social action, Martin Luther King Jr. advocated that authentic Christian religion must not only be concerned with ultimate reality—for example, questions of heaven, eternity, transcendence—but also with the social conditions in which black people must live. Although eschatological hope is an aspect of the black religious experience, it makes little sense to speak of otherworldliness to the man victimized by the iron hand of poverty and deprivation who is fighting an endless battle for mere survival. The new dimension to which I refer—the "engagement" motif—is astutely symbolized in the theological and ethical orientation of Martin Luther King. Jr.

For King, authentic Christian religion must operate at both the vertical and horizontal levels of human existence, if we are to be free for ourselves, our neighbor, and our God. From a socioethical perspective, authentic Christian religion must engage persons in the struggle against the forces that affect the quality of human life. These forces, in the ethical thought of King, were reflected in a system of segregation, dehumanization, and oppression of black people in the larger society. Authentic Christian religion ought to speak to these social conditions. In his book *Stride toward Freedom,* King states:

> Any religion that professes to be concerned with the souls of men and is not concerned with the slums that damn them, the economic conditions that strangle them, and the social conditions that cripple them, is a dry-as-dust religion. Such a religion is the kind that Marxists like to see—an opiate of the people![10]

Two Prophets to White America

Any cursory glance at the literature in either rap culture or European American public life would undoubtedly suggest that the philosophy and ethics of Martin and Malcolm played a vital role in shaping the lives of black people during the turbulent decade of the 1960s. In assessing the far-reaching impacts of Malcolm and Martin in the realm of black culture, James Cone in *Martin and Malcolm and America: A Dream or a Nightmare* has rightly observed:

> The first area to consider is black culture and consciousness. Though both men participated in this realm, Malcolm was the towering figure. He was a cultural revolutionary who almost singlehandedly transformed the way black people thought about themselves. He was the progenitor of the black consciousness movement that emerged during the 1960s, affecting the whole of black life, including art (black aesthetics), education (black studies), politics (Black Power), and religion (black theology).[11]

The power and force of these African American personalities can be seen in their ability, intellectually, to use the art of language and the spoken word the way an artist wields a paintbrush. As naturally as breathing fresh air or drinking cold water, Martin and Malcolm used the power of oratory to recover the moral fragments and spiritual remnants of black culture, which inspired African Americans to think black, buy black, sleep black, love black, and act black! Why? Because our blackness is who we are; it is our battle-ax in the struggle for freedom and equality; it is the nursery of self-esteem for the young and old; and it is the legacy of our foreparents, who proverbially taught us that "it takes a village to raise a child."

For Martin and Malcolm, blackness is nothing less than the playground of being that energizes people of color to transcend the imposed false feelings of inadequacy, inferiority, or hopelessness, so often affixed and strapped on the backs of the poor and oppressed. For Malcolm and Martin, the reality of blackness is derived from the African experience and the religio-cultural heritage, which proverbially teaches us that "only those who have been tried in the fire will not scorch in the sun" and that a "spider's web united can tie up a lion!" For Martin and Malcolm, the reality of blackness is the essential glue that holds together one's sense of cultural integrity, religious strength, and humanity.

In the lives of both Martin and Malcolm, one can imagine the rhythmic echo of Aretha Franklin singing, "Respect . . . just a little bit!" or James Brown shouting, "Say it loud . . . I'm black and I'm proud!" As a theologian and a minister, Martin believed that all of the fancy and positive talk about blackness and the black-is-beautiful philosophy could not replace the basic need for love, as human beings living in the world—regardless of race, creed, color, gender, or religious persuasion. From the viewpoint of methodology, while Malcolm's philosophy seems to be a sort of Afrocentric cultural nationalism, Martin's is more likely to portray the self and the world in terms of the universal yearnings of all people for love, acceptance, and affirmation.

In King's classic work *Where Do We Go from Here: Chaos or Community?* he spoke of love as a call and as a unifying principle that transcends race, religion, and class boundaries:

> This call for a world-wide fellowship that lifts neighborly concern beyond one's tribe, race, class and nation is in reality a call for an all-embracing and unconditional love for all men. This often misunderstood and misinterpreted concept has now become an absolute necessity for the survival of man. When I speak of love, I am speaking of that force which all the great religions have seen as the supreme unifying principle of life. Love is the key that unlocks the door which leads to ultimate reality.[12]

Now as a necessary ingredient undergirding the Million Man March, we shall return to this notion of love as the integrative core of human life. Meanwhile, we must identify a functional conceptual framework that may serve as a theoretical tool of understanding in exploring the differences in style, critical method, and life orientation between Martin and Malcolm on the critical issues of authentic freedom and racial justice in America.

Different Approaches, Same Goal

The renowned sociologist C. Eric Lincoln analyzes the different approaches used by iconic leaders like Martin and Malcolm in understanding black suffering and racism in the United States. In his celebrated book *The Black Church in the African American Experience,* Lincoln describes these different approaches or interpretive schemes as the dialectical model of the black sacred cosmos.[13] Although Lincoln and his colleague Lawrence H. Mamiya were looking primarily at the black church experience in America, the contrasting models summarized include the following:

1. The assimilation model—the main view in this model is the belief in the necessity of the demise of the black church as a social institution for the public good of blacks, in light of the dominant values of integration into the mainstream of American life. For instance, assimilationists tend to see the black church as radically anti-intellectual and authoritarian.

2. The isolation model—this is a view of the black church experience characterized by "involuntary isolation," which is due largely to the socioeconomic factors of poverty, poor education, and inadequate health care for the oppressed and lower-class folks, who may perceive the role of religion in human society as being primarily otherworldly.

3. The compensatory model—according to Lincoln and Mamiya, the main attraction of the black church here is to provide the masses with opportunity and access to power, position, status, control, and social rank within the ethnic body itself, which they do not ordinarily receive in the wider society. The authors cite St. Clair Drake and Horace Cayton, in their book *Black Metropolis*, as an illustration of this model. Of course, the classic work of Mays and Nicholson, *The Negro's God*, could logically be included under this conceptual framework.

4. The ethnic community–prophetic model—this particular approach gives a more wholesome and constructive interpretation of the black church experience in American society. It seems to emphasize the importance of "building a sense of ethnic identity and a community of interest among its members."[14]

For Lincoln, the purpose of the dialectical model of the black sacred cosmos is to provide some social analysis of the historical experience of black suffering in America and to better understand the role of religion in the spiritual and cultural formation of black identity.[15] Lincoln asserts that there are six "main pairs of dialectically related tensions in his model, which have implications for better understanding of the legacy of Martin Luther King Jr. and Malcolm X. These briefly include the following:"

(a) the dialectic between priestly and prophetic functions;
(b) the dialectic between otherworldly versus this-worldly;
(c) the dialectic between universalism and particularism;
(d) the dialectic between the communal and the privatistic;
(e) the dialectic between charismatic versus bureaucratic; and
(f) the dialectic between resistance versus accommodation.[16]

These six pairs of dialectical polarities may give the reader a more comprehensive theoretical background and understanding of both Martin and Malcolm and how their different approaches to the problems of black suffering and identity in America actually set the stage for the Million Man March. Hence, I want to strongly suggest that Malcolm's conceptual approach to black life in America seems to resemble the isolationist–separatist model as expressive of Lincoln's topology, whereas Martin's conceptual approach tends to reflect the assimilationist–integrationist approach, which emphasizes the popular themes or slogans of the civil rights movement such as "Black and White Together," "Love Your Enemies," "Nonviolence as a Way of Life," "First-Class Citizenship," "We Shall Overcome"—to name only a few. By comparison and contrast, Malcolm's ideological approach to the plight of blacks living in America seems to reflect such values and sentiments as "separate, not integrated," "self-defense," "self-help," "black ownership," "black by nature, proud by choice," and the famous rallying cry that black people will—inevitably—gain their freedom "by any means necessary!"

Perhaps herein lies the sharpest contrast between Martin's philosophy of aggressive nonviolent love or love monism as strategy for social change and Malcolm's philosophy of black cultural nationalism as strategy—but always facing the ethical problematic of "by any means necessary." When confronted by a difficult problem in the community, what does it mean to say, "By any means necessary"? Should means and ends be consistent and morally coherent? On the other hand, what does it mean for the ethically sensitive person to utter, "Love your enemy!"? Who is my enemy? Am I thinking clearly about what or where the enemy is? Is the so-called enemy internal or external in relation to the public good of the black community?

These are ethically serious questions we must ponder in light of the theological and philosophical roots of both Martin and Malcolm. Although their approaches differ, these two modern prophets had the same goal for the sons and daughters of Africa: authentic freedom, equality, respect, and the love of God and neighbor.

Is There Common Ground?

As we look at the questions of vision and common purpose for human liberation, where do we find common ground in the critical moral philosophy of El Hajj Malik el Shabazz and Martin Luther King Jr.? What contributions have they made to America in lifting the veil of racial bigotry and ignorance? In *Martin, Malcolm, and America,* James Cone states that the white media have too long kept apart these two brothers—these two champions of justice who took separate roads to the Promised Land. He asserts that because Martin was the darling of the white liberal establishment in the public eye, he got good press; and because Malcolm was depicted as the militant rebel of black nationalism, he got bad press. Thus Cone's questions are relevant: How should we understand the meaning of Martin and Malcolm for each other? What similarities are worth remembering?

First, the historical record shows that both leaders fought and died for the same basic goal: freedom. The ethical notion of freedom meant—during the civil rights movement of the 1960s— freedom from discrimination and insult, freedom from segregation and moral degradation, and freedom from feelings of inferiority, powerlessness, and solitude. Though the pathways and methods were different, the goal was always the same. For example, Malcolm made this point explicit about his work when he said, "Dr. King wants the same thing that I want—freedom!"

Second, we may observe that during their years of social struggle in American society they had different methods of achieving human dignity and the ultimate goal. For Martin, the concept of integration came to symbolize this viable method, undergirded by the Gandhian philosophy of nonviolent resistance. For Malcolm, the concept of separation became the overarching philosophical method for achieving the ultimate goal. Here Malcolm was more likely to argue that freedom for outcast and oppressed blacks must come "by any means necessary." For instance, Malcolm makes this point explicit in his speech "The Ballot or the Bullet" when he says—regarding Martin's nonviolent approach—"I'm not for separation and you're not for integration. What you and I are for is freedom. Only you think that integration will get you freedom; I think separation will get me free. We both have the same objective. We've just got different ways of getting at it."

Third, Martin's integrationist orientation as a civil rights leader would more likely emphasize social acceptance and accommodation in a multicultural society, whereas Malcolm's ethical inclination seems to stress respect as human beings—with a deep sensitivity to the religio-cultural heritage of Africa.

Fourth, Martin's religious orientation was deeply shaped not only by the social gospel movement, neoorthodoxy, and the Boston University School of personalism, but also by the faith of the black church. For Malcolm the language of faith was shaped by the Nation of Islam and the moral teachings of the Honorable Elijah Muhammad, which tended to personify the ideology of blackness. In one sense, the legacy of Martin was that he was a prophet of love and justice; by contrast, Malcolm was a prophet of truth and a new consciousness on the part of African Americans. For young black men, I am inclined to agree with Ossie Davis's assessment of Malcolm as "Our Own Shining Black Prince."[17]

Be that as it may, I hold the conviction that both Malcolm and Martin were "transformed nonconformists," in the sense that they expanded our vision of social justice and human rights by refusing to accept white definitions of black life in America and by refusing to be used as doormats in America in the shell game of white racism. If we really are to find common ground for tomorrow, we must learn how to hope and to dream again. Maybe not to dream the American dream in a conventional way, because of its tendency toward cultural imperialism, but rather to recognize that everyone has feelings, spiritual yearnings, instincts, ethical sensibilities, and dreams to sell in the vast economy of God's creation. The spirit of the Million Man March would have us remember that everyone is a roaming shopper for dreams in a brave new world. Here are some of my own thoughts about this:

Did You Get the Point

The point is not
Finding a perfect role model
To imitate but really
Being who you are;
The point is not
Intellect over character
But intellect through
Character.

The point is not
The evil of hatred in
Our world but
The transcendence of love
Over our world;
The point is not
The love of power
But the power of love.

The point is not
A peace that passeth
All understanding but
An understanding
Laced-with-justice that
Brings peace; therefore,
The Point is not
Desire over reason,
But desire tempered
By reason.[18]

Suffering Love Meets Afrophobia and Europhobia

As seekers of truth and freedom, we should never let go of our dreams. Dreams empower us to embrace "suffering love," which enables the people of faith to overcome adversity and the burdens of Afrophobia and Europhobia in ethnic relations. We are challenged, as the sons and daughters of the Million Man March, to dare to dream a world yet unborn, but which must be—if we are to be truly free. We are challenged to achieve the highest good and deepest faith in the heart and soul of African Americans in contemporary society. But what is suffering love all about?

Suffering love is not the absence of conflict or tension in human relationships but the presence of justice and respect. Love is justice distributed. In any event, when suffering love meets xenophobic situations, things happen. When suffering love meets Afrophobia and Europhobia face to face, a transformation takes place. In the arena of human conflict and struggle between black and white, rich and poor, and the haves and have-nots, the reality of suffering love makes a difference. The morally sensitive person might simply ask, "What is Afrophobia or Europhobia in light of our reflections on the legacy of the Million Man March?" Well, to ask a question implies getting a reasonable response.

In my booklet *Living at the Intersection of Race and Religion,* I agonized over the importance of these generative concepts as critical dimensions in one's understanding of the diverse philosophies of both Martin and Malcolm. Thus in the parlance of ethnic relations, *Afrophobia* is a concept referring literally to fear of people of African descent; *Europhobia* refers to fear of people of European descent.

Our analysis of Martin and Malcolm implies that we as American citizens have a lot of growing to do politically, culturally, and spiritually on both sides of what W. E. B. DuBois called the "color line." Put another way, the great nineteenth-century songwriter and moral philosopher James Weldon Johnson once remarked, "The race problem in America involves the saving of the Black America's body and the white America's soul."[19] Whether you agree or disagree, the truth of the matter is simple, yet awesome: the power of suffering love implicit in the critical thought of Martin and Malcolm has the capacity to overcome the negative forces of Afrophobia and Europhobia.

Suffering love is unconditional. Suffering love is redemptive. Suffering love is transformative in its power to do a new thing in majority–minority relations in America. But suffering love always begins—pragmatically—with African Americans taking responsibility for their own actions, attitudes, resources, dreams, and spiritual values as blacks, more from the "anger" of self-pity to moral agency and self-determination.[20] In short, I suspect that this is a key normative element in the legacy of both Martin and Malcolm as a backdrop for understanding the ideological dynamics of the Million Man March.

Ethically considered, suffering love is nothing less than what is required by the gospel of Jesus Christ as a community of faith, namely, to love one another as sisters and brothers of the human family of God, to embrace the ontological beauty and paradox of our own blackness, to fervently work for the increase of justice and peace among inner-city neighborhoods torn by violence and despair, and to affirm the African heritage that reminds us that it takes a village to raise a child.

Suffering love is the unifying vision implicit in the philosophy and theology of both Martin and Malcolm that gives us the capacity to dream about a world where the poor and hurting ones can find relief from exploitation and oppression as well as acceptance and affirmation in human community. Indeed, I dream a world wherein the baker will speak about the Living Bread. I dream a world wherein the artist will image the Chief Architect of the Universe. I dream a world where the banker will not be a profit hog or capitalist broker for Wall Street but a beneficent broker of the hidden treasure of God's realm. I dream a world where the educator will once again teach and inspire moral and spiritual values in youth and adults alike. I dream a world wherein the builder will not be content until the fragile soul of every human being can rest upon the Sure Foundation. I dream a world wherein the poor and homeless are not turned away and despised because of their wretchedness but are embraced because of God's righteousness. I dream a world beyond black and white, wherein diversity is celebrated as a gift and not a burden. Yes, sisters and brothers, I dream a world big enough ideologically for Martin and Malcolm, for David Walker and Nat Turner, Frederick Douglass and John Brown, W. E. B. DuBois and Booker T. Washington, Harriet Tubman and Mary McLeod Bethune, Maya Angelou and Angela Davis, Louis Farrakhan and Colin Powell, Tiger Woods and Michael Jordan—to name only a few.

Suffering love gives the moral agent the imagination and wisdom to dream a world wherein the lamb need not fear the lion as they roam and find food to eat in a common pasture. Suffering love energizes the moral agent to dream a world wherein the lamb not only lies down with the lion, but where the lamb's getting up again is guaranteed! In the final analysis, I suspect that what we find in the critical thought patterns of both Martin and Malcolm is an intellectually diverse legacy that provides the reader with an interpretive scheme for understanding the Million Man March phenomenon.

Poetically, it was all about how to dream a world wherein the politics of suffering love swallows up the demons of fear and renders dysfunctional the meandering clouds of Afrophobia and Europhobia that impede our common struggle for full equality and liberation as a whole people of God. Therefore, let us not fear or grow weary about the ambiguities, racial antipathies, and moral contradictions of history. Ultimately, the politics of suffering love is expressed powerfully in the Bible: "So let us not grow weary in doing what is right, for we will reap in harvest-time, if we do not give up" (Galatians 6:9). Indeed, the politics of suffering love for the daughters and sons of the Million Man March requires that we embrace such love in its perfect form. As the Holy Scriptures teach, "There is no fear in love; but perfect love casteth out fear" (1 John 4:18).

Open Letter from Brotha to Sister

I WILL NEVER AGAIN USE THE "B WORD" TO DESCRIBE ANY FEMALE.
BUT PARTICULARLY MY OWN BLACK SISTER. I PLEDGE FROM THIS DAY
FORWARD THAT I WILL NOT POISON MY BODY WITH DRUGS OR THAT
WHICH IS DESTRUCTIVE TO MY HEALTH AND MY WELL-BEING.
—The Million Man March Pledge

WHEN YOU EDUCATE A MAN, YOU EDUCATE AN INDIVIDUAL, BUT
WHEN YOU EDUCATE A WOMAN, YOU EDUCATE A NATION.
—Johnnetta B. Cole

Dearly Beloved Sister,

Beloved Sister, I believe that one of the implicit learnings from
the Million Man March is the affirmation of the beauty of black
womanhood. I give thanks to the Creator for your inner beauty
and strength. I give thanks to the Creator for your integrity and
willingness to tell me the truth about me. Yes, you might say that
this "truth thing" concerning who I am is a baffling question that
I feel more comfortable denying than facing. But Sister, you have
a way of cutting through the core of my psychological props and
defenses, and therefore getting at the heart of the matter.

Beloved Sister, I am disturbed and concerned that as I observe
the journalistic musings of the mass media about the issue of
women of color, there is very little that's praiseworthy. It seems to
me that the dominant media is hung up on the "good girl/bad
girl" image or the "welfare queen" image of African American
women in this society. I suspect that what this image implies in

the wider society is, in the words of Aretha Franklin, that women of color "don't get no respect"! But you see, my sister, I have an image problem too, in this country we call America. My image problem didn't start with me so much as with otherness. That is to say, the dominant host culture writes its own script of my image—whether that image takes the form of a "superfly," "common criminal," "mugger," "violent perpetrator," "thief," or "lazy freeloader," I am still portrayed, invariably, as something less than who I am.

Beloved Sister, the upshot of this little scenario is the inner awareness that before I can work on my own "image in the culture," I've gotta tune in to how we both have been given a bad rap in a society not fully of our own making. But let me say from the outset that in the spirit of the Million Man March, we really need to talk *to* each other, rather than *at* each other. We need to talk to each other, not so much in the psychology of dialogue between male and female, but rather in the ethics of love as brother and sister on a common journey toward healing and wholeness. Though touched by the burdens of racial injustice and pain in our world, there is still a bond of friendship that runs, like a river, deep in our veins. Our bond requires honesty and open conversation. As our beloved sister Alice Walker once observed, "No person is your friend who demands your silence, or denies your right to grow."[1]

Beloved Sister, let us not stand in each other's shadow, but let us not fail to recognize and to share in each other's pain. You see, my sister, while I have much to atone for, I also have much to be grateful for. For example, concerning the countless seminars, workshops, and gatherings I have attended over the last three years around the theme "Improving Male–Female Relationships," one is likely to echo the famous words of Fannie Lou Hamer, who said, "I'm sick and tired of being sick and tired!" By this I mean to suggest that most folks I know in the churches, lodges, and gathering places in the black community are fed up with talk and dialogue. What about action and result? When do we get around to doing what we talk? Or is it just that: all talk and no walk? Let's not fool ourselves. The shining stars of our collective struggle of the past knew not only how to talk the talk, but also how to walk the walk. They knew how to struggle together as brothers and sisters for freedom and a common purpose, to alleviate the plight of people who live on the ragged edges of survival.

Beloved Sister, the problem nowadays is that our struggle appears to be less communal and more individualistic. We seem to embrace more commonly the philosophy of self-aggrandizement which says, "You only go around once in life, so grab for all the gusto." As long as we are in this culture, we will have to grapple, I believe, with this brand of Americanism and possessive individualism. So Sister, while I atone for my private sins toward you—whether they take the form of abuse, hurt, or deception—I still know in my gut that's not the whole story. We must not, I believe, lose sight of the big picture. Let me, therefore, be as clear as my mind can be. The bottom line is, we need one another.

Beloved Sister, I don't need you behind me to push, but rather beside me to support me with the strength of your unconditional love.

Beloved Sister, I don't need you to remind me daily of my bad habits, faults, and failures because they are as numerous as the sands of time. The white system of control in America has done a mighty good job at that. But I feel in my soul and straight from my heart that what I need from you is this:

- I need you to remind me of the tough garment of self-determination.

- I need you to remind me of my own armor of courage in the struggle against apathy and nihilism in the black community.
- I need you, my beloved, to remind me of the shield of faith and my own inner loyalty to the God-force, which empowers us all to do the right thing.

From brotha to sister, I boldly proclaim that our only real weapon for survival in America is an uncompromising commitment to truth, an uncompromising commitment to our children, and the pursuit of excellence in whatever things we do on this planet. For nothing less will satisfy, nothing more is needed.

Beloved Sister, although we live daily with the conditions of oppression, it is still, I believe, within our power to rise above any circumstances. Nobody will deny that the circumstances of our existence in American society are varied and complex. But there are steps we may take to survive and improve upon our condition. Now what follows are some practical steps or items to be included in the survival kit for the future:

1. From brotha to sister, I believe and affirm that our children are our future. Sister, my beloved, what I am trying to say is simple yet awesome: The community is the foundational nursery for the care and nurture of our children. Sister, my beloved, I believe that no child should be outside the care of this foundational nursery. You must remember, my sister, that from the perspective of Old Country, African people of Tanzania—under the former prophetic leadership of Julius K. Nyerere—would use the word *Ujamaa* to describe this notion of the extended family. The Swahili word *Ujamaa* literally means "familyhood." We don't have to become the highest achiever in our class or to attend Harvard

University in order to qualify for membership in the extended family; you don't have to be of a certain color, social rank, or class in order to have standing in the extended family. Beloved Sister, you don't have to become uppity or elitist in order to qualify for membership in the extended family, but rather, the notion of Ujamaa includes all children and all people unconditionally. But I think that must be one of the key items in the survival kit for our neighborhood children. For example, Jesus loved little children so much he made them the normative example for the realm of God (Matthew 19:14).

2. From brotha to sister, I believe and affirm that in order for our children to survive the criminal element in society, parents and adults must empower them to distinguish between "trash" and "treasure." Remember, I say to you, "Young mothers, . . . you teenage mothers, raise your children with love, to believe in themselves, teach them positive things. . . . Let them know early on in life, that when God created them . . . God didn't create no 'junk' or 'trash.'" Beloved Sister, what is at stake in your relation to me is how we see and care for these little precious treasures we call our babies.

But Sister, as you know, one of the big problems among black teens is the whole out-of-control phenomenon of babies having babies! Beloved Sister, I must honestly tell you that my heartbeat quickens when I think about the menacing threat of teen pregnancy and its impact on the quality of child-rearing practices and moral values in the black community.

Beloved Sister, I write this letter to you because I feel way down in my soul that our community leaders, social workers, educators, administrators, preachers, parents, and public servants from all walks of life must get a handle on the critical problem of teen pregnancy. Sister, I beg you to ponder with me the issues of strategy and the ethics of care. For example, what sort of community-based strategies seem feasible in addressing the plague of teen pregnancy in urban America? What specific role should religious institutions or civic organizations play in the critical process of planning? In terms of the strategy to combat teen pregnancy, what is the cost of care? What is the cost of neglect? How can we engender positive self-esteem among our teenagers so they won't see themselves as trash but treasure? Beloved Sister, these are some of the hard questions that swell up inside of me when I think about a survival kit for the future of those who will come after us.

Beloved Sister, we must emphatically declare to each teenager, "Accept yourself as God made you—beautiful, strong, generative, hardworking, and intelligent." While current research shows that American teens seem to get pregnant at a higher rate than those from other industrialized countries of the West, it does not logically follow that black teens must be slaves to reckless sexual behavior and reproductive patterns. The upshot of the "trash-or-treasure" metaphor is the recognition that each teenager—male and female—must be responsible for his or her own sexual behavior, despite the heavy influence of peer pressure and the good and bad choices we sometimes make.[2]

3. From brotha to sister, I believe and affirm that when others put you down, God will pick you up. Beloved Sister, as I write this letter to you I need not remind you, too strongly, of the wisdom implicit in this moral precept. For whatever reason, people will, from time to time, try and dump on you. We as humans have a peculiar egocentric habit of dumping on each other, of using other folks as a doormat. Perhaps the social critics and political realists of human nature and its institutions would say

that this impulse to dump or put others down satisfies the need for power and security in an increasingly fragmented and insecure world. Perhaps it is a mere form of socialization tied in with the struggle to survive in the jungles of modern society. Obviously, I don't know the source of this peculiar impulse, but we all seem to have it.

Beloved Sister, the alternative to the sin of dumping is the wisdom of grace. God's grace picks us up when others put us down. The gift of grace lifts the heavy loads we must bear. Grace regenerates. Grace renews. Grace transforms. Grace endures all things, even the sufferings and cruel contradictions of history. Beloved Sister, I remember reading in my Bible that when people try and put us down, we must then "consider him that endured such hostility against himself from sinners, so that you may not grow weary or lose heart" (Hebrews 12:3). You see, my sister, we must believe deep within that when others play the game of putting us down, there is a God-force that can pick us up.

Beloved Sister, I write you to say that when the windstorms of life blow hard against your face, don't stop striving to be all you can be, but ask God to place the windstorm at your back. You see, my sister, every battle we encounter starts first in the mind. The Bible teaches us to remember that as we think in our heart, so are we (Proverbs 23:7). Here it seems to me that the whole matter starts with the mind and how we struggle morally and spiritually to reason things through—in order to curb the tendency of putting others down. In short, my beloved sister, I believe and affirm that reason is the voice of the mind, faith is the voice of the heart, and conscience is the voice of the human spirit.

4. From brotha to sister, I believe and affirm that while we live daily with the conditions of oppression, it is within our power to

rise above any circumstance. The legacy of the African heritage challenges us to recover the spirit of the eagle. That is to say, my sister, to recover a sense of self-transcendence. The language of self-transcendence is the language of soaring. I mean that we can rise above the difficulties and hard circumstances of life.

Of course, as I write this letter to you, some folks will undoubtedly say that the Million Man March was just a big show of egoism on a national stage, between controversial personalities that brought us to the edge of communal chaos and destruction. Others may lament loudly that we are already faced with a dual moral dilemma: the problem of the color line, which has divided our nation for centuries, and the problem of the ideology line, which draws a wedge between Christians and Muslims and between integrationists and separatists. Here some believe that African Americans are literally on the edge of unreconciled ideological conflict. Maybe or maybe not. Yet I say to you—as a participant in the Million Man March—that the ideological climate of the day felt to me more like the movement of the Spirit that brought us to the edge of healing rather than to the edge of hostility. It felt more like the movement of the Spirit that brought us closer to confluence than to conflict. The element we have called self-transcendence is a marvelous thing, my sister, because it refuses to allow others—black or white—to define our boundaries or to put a muzzle on our destiny. In the poetic words of DeLois C. Nance, the bare essence of self-transcendence is captured as she talks about the struggles of blacks in the land of the free. Her poem "America" is directed toward people of goodwill who refuse to allow their dreams to be fenced in:

Don't get fenced in; don't be tied down.
Help plan your destiny.

Don't be told where you cannot pray.
Let's keep our great land free.

Help choose the ones to lead this land,
Your right to vote is free.
Together we will help to plan
And keep our great land free.[3]

Well, Sister, I must move on now. Certainly, there are other things I need to say to you, but the demands of time will not allow me. Certainly I need to tell you that I've done a lot of mean and cruel things to you through the years for which I am sorry. Please be patient with me, because God ain't finished with me. I am still making mistakes, but I'm still growing—spiritually and intellectually—and together we will plan our destiny.

Sincerely,

Your Soul Brotha

Telling the Stories of Black Culture

BOTH MYTH AND RITUAL PROVIDE CULTURAL SOLUTIONS TO PROB-
LEMS WHICH ALL HUMAN BEINGS FACE. HUMAN BEINGS BUILD THEIR
CULTURES, NERVOUSLY LOQUACIOUS, UPON THE EDGE OF AN ABYSS.

—William A. Lessa

SOME PEOPLE ARE YOUR RELATIVES BUT OTHERS ARE YOUR
ANCESTORS, AND YOU CHOOSE THE ONES YOU WANT TO HAVE AS
ANCESTORS. YOU CREATE YOURSELF OUT OF THOSE VALUES.

—Ralph Ellison

In the religion and culture of African people, the concept of myth is
not the ideological equivalent of that which is false as opposed to that
which is true, but rather a reality that impinges upon our consciousness so strongly that we cannot escape.[1] The concept of myth is a far
more complex element in the creative web of religion and culture.
Myth is about self-creation. It means many things to different people in the continuous search for meaning and purpose in the puz-
zle we call life. The desire to find meaning, purpose, and freedom
is never a simple possibility for the inquiring mind. Because life is
tough and paradoxical, man is a problem unto himself. Woman is
a problem unto herself. Each child, though endowed with beauty
and limitless potential, is a problem unto himself or herself. In
short, the individual as moral agent constitutes a problem, because
the road of life itself is marked by tempting parking spaces.

The use of myths is a powerful mode of storytelling; it becomes
a way of making sense out of human experience and claiming

one's own identity. Myth plays a vital role in this sociohistorical process of recovery and self-authentification. Adults and children in the African American community are, therefore, compelled by racism in the United States to understand the boundaries of their culture and recover their history as a people of God by exploring the mythopoetic stories.[2]

Myth and Divinity

Charles E. Morton, noted black professor of philosophy at Howard University, in his informative book *The Ideological Character of Moral Judgment,* makes the following bold assertion regarding the value of mythology:

> Mythology was used as an ideological device to express moral conviction and direct social behavior in the early civilizations of Egypt, Mesopotamia and Greece. The myths of these civilizations reflect convictions held about events, vital powers, and forces believed operative in the total context of life that were symbolic of a reality that had to be conceptualized and adjusted to appropriately. In early societies these vital forces were individualized and personified. Eventually, all the processes and experiences of real importance to the individual and the social group became gods.[3]

This learned black philosopher goes on to suggest to the reader that the notion of myth is tied in to one's understanding of divinity. Indeed, Morton observes that in ancient African culture there is no theoretical separation between mythic structures of human life and the practice of religion. The two are organically interrelated as images of God were projected for nearly everything pertaining to the phenomenon of creation itself—fertility, love, hate, happiness, success, and well-being in the universe.

The myth was a way of inviting each believer to stand before the divine court of God and to confess the things done in life and to see if they measure up to God's concerns for righteousness, love, deliverance, and peace over all the earth. To be sure, this notion of the mythopoetic structure of human existence provides us valuable insight into the creation narrative of ancient Egyptian culture and religion. The myth also gives us who live in contemporary American society a clue as to how God anointed certain leaders such as Harriet Tubman, Frederick Douglass, Marcus Garvey, Martin Luther King Jr., and Malcolm X to lead marginalized people out of the degradation of slavery into the promise of freedom.

This moral perspective suggests to the ordinary reader that the ancient creation myths about freedom from human bondage still have relevance for African Americans today, especially in light of the spirit of the Million Man March. Concerning the power of ancient creation mythology, Morton gives this summary:

> The creation myth already reflects the centralization of power that existed in the Pharaoh during the Old Kingdom period of Egypt. But when the nobles who ruled the "nomes" (small areas) resisted subordination to the Pharaohs of the Middle Kingdom period, this myth was employed by writers to develop what has come to be called Memphite Theology—a mythological system in which Egypt is the vassalage of the Pharaoh who in turn is god's appointed king to rule on earth.[4]

Mythopoetic Stories

The value of the myth is storytelling in the lived world of experiences—as people of African descent attempt to communicate with each other and to construct a faith system that transcends the cancer of racism in America. The myth may communicate—through the individual or social group—a moral ideology that empowers us to struggle with the trials and tribulations, burdens and pains, and heartbreaks and contradictions of human existence. For the religiously devout person, therefore, the myth can function as an ideological device to order our steps into the deepness of God.

Given the moral tone of the religiously devout person as mythologist, we can affirm that life has meaning and purpose—despite the perennial burdens of racism and oppression in America—because of who God is. For example, the basic faith claim nurtured in our children must be this: "Life is difficult, but God is good!" God the merciful and beneficent can order our steps into the pathway of truth. Indeed, many anthropological studies show that the ancient African mythologists were ordinary men and women who searched tenaciously for wisdom and truth.

In retrospect, I was amused and struck by the thousands of individuals who simply showed up on the Mall in Washington, D.C., on that divinely appointed mythopoetic day, Monday, October 16, 1995. It seems to me that one of the powerful lessons to be learned from this special day of atonement is the value of affirming the truth and wisdom from within the heart and soul of black people universally. Each individual—men and women, boys and girls, babies in strollers, babies strapped to their mother's backs—who dared simply to show up made a powerful statement and set a moral tone. On this seemingly endless day of atonement, each individual took on the role of the mythologist. To be black, living in America, as the dawn of the new millennium dawns, means embracing the role of the mythologist. What I am trying to suggest here is simply that the African American as mythologist is one who no longer looks first to Europe in the search for wisdom and truth, but to Africa, the mother and cradle of civilization.

The Story of the Grasshopper

African American people are a storytelling people. Stories entertain, instruct, and guide us along life's journey. The art of storytelling gives to our faith legs to walk with and eyes to see with. There could be no sense of moral tradition, cultural values, and biblical legacy without the role of the mythologist as storyteller. The stories we tell to one another mirror self-esteem and anchor one's faith in the community.

Therefore, we come now to a second story that seems to reveal the mythopoetic dimensions of our common life as a people engaged in the struggle for true freedom and equality in the United States. Ironically, we may say that the story of the grasshopper is the idiom and folklore of African American culture and may disclose something about ourselves that we may not want to face. It is especially difficult for any oppressed people to engage meaningfully in the art of internal self-criticism—whether the conversation is about how we look, smell, think, pray, or behave. In respect to human nature and society, we human beings seem to be more prone to see others' faults rather than our own.

In black folklore, the story of the grasshopper is the amazing tale of one who has a narrow vision of the world, which obscures a people's true greatness. Etymologically speaking, the term *myosis* refers to a condition of the eyes that inhibits one from seeing and thinking clearly. The word's more specific medical definition is "any abnormal contraction of the pupil of the eye."

Metaphorically, the notion of myosis for the African American religious person means that one's moral vision is shown to be obstructed and off center. Before we plunge head-on into the narrative of the grasshopper, however, we raise hard ethical questions: What can the Bible teach us about the dangers of myopic or limited vision? What is the source of our moral vision for the oppressed black community? How do we think about thinking as a people with shared memories of suffering and hope in white America?

Black people in this nation as well as in the global society cry out for an answer to these and other pertinent moral concerns. A logical place to begin religious discussion is with the principle of critical thinking; that is, the Bible engages the believer to pay attention to attitude before taking action in its effect upon the Christian moral life. Did not the Bible, as the living Word of God, remind the believer that "as a man thinks in his heart, so is he" (Proverbs 23:7)? The Scriptures proclaim, "Keep your heart with all vigilance; for from it flow the springs of life" (Proverbs 4:23). For African Americans, I believe that right thinking is the precondition to genuine moral vision in the society in which we live, move, and have our being.

As we shall see, the problem with the grasshopper tale is one of distorted vision as a result of past social conditioning. Now in the mythopoetic structure of storytelling, we shall call this tale the modern Afrocentric parable of "Tom, the Grasshopper."

Once upon a time, before Tom, the Grasshopper, became "Tom," he would spend many joyous hours in the deep green forest without a care in the world. As the modern parable unravels, we observe that Tom, the Grasshopper—without warning or intent—fell into a large jar, with an automatic lid on top. There he stayed for over 250 years until his friend, Hodges, came along and took the lid off the top of the jar. Having become conditioned by the lid, Tom was unaware that the lid was actually off and subsequently stayed within the jar for another 100 years. You see, Tom, the Grasshopper, had become socially adjusted to the environment inside—a painful price for survival!

Finally, there came along in due time another friend, the moral force, and he said:

Hey, Tom! Hey, Tom! Way down there, don't you know the lid is off the jar . . . ? Hop on out, man, into the land of freedom! You need not be bound by the false lid. You really are free. Praise God! Hallelujah! Hallelujah! The chains have been broken from your legs and mind forever. Hop on out![5]

The Story of a Yoke and a Water Jug

This story of our reflections on the mythopoetic dimension of life is a story about the obligation or "yoke" to give something back to the community. Human life is not always about what we can get, but what we give and do for others less fortunate. The Bible, as well as the Holy Koran, set a high value on the yoke of self-giving. It has been said, and some believe, that the "yoke" symbolizes a burden, but it can also symbolize a blessing through the eyes of faith. It carries both responsibility and the moral mandate to follow that which is good in human community. For example, let us listen to the words of Jesus concerning the yoke: "Take my yoke upon you and learn from me; for I am gentle and humble in heart, and you will find rest for your souls. For my yoke is easy, and my burden is light" (Matthew 11:29–30). Hence, the mythopoetic implication of yoke is the call to responsibility and the invitation to leave something behind.

This brings us to our exciting story about the jug. Once upon a time, two men got lost in the sub-Saharan desert of East Africa while on a safari. In the course of two days, they were out of water and food and in a state of destitution and great peril. After some sleepless nights, they saw a brightly colored jug stuck in the hot sand far in the distance. The jug was filled to the brim with clean water. They danced and rejoiced and sang praises to God for the saving water. It literally saved their lives! But on the outside of the jug there was a small inscription that read: "Did you leave any water in the jug for the thirsty sojourner who will come after you?"

It seems to me that this is the main question or lesson of the Million Man March. What did we take back home? What are we involved with in the local community? Are we taking up the yoke of service and love for the poor and hurting ones? Listen up, you brothers and sisters, are we leaving any water in the jug for those who will follow?

Open Letter from Brotha to God

AND I HEARD A LOUD VOICE FROM THE THRONE SAYING, SEE, THE
HOME OF GOD IS AMONG MORTALS. HE WILL DWELL WITH THEM AS
THEIR GOD; THEY WILL BE HIS PEOPLES, AND GOD HIMSELF WILL
BE WITH THEM; HE WILL WIPE EVERY TEAR FROM THEIR EYES.
DEATH WILL BE NO MORE; MOURNING AND CRYING AND PAIN WILL
BE NO MORE, FOR THE FIRST THINGS HAVE PASSED AWAY.

—Revelation 21:3–4

Dear God,

This letter is sent marked priority mail and overnight express
to heaven's post office. I was told by the principalities and powers
on earth that you probably would not accept this letter because of
insufficient postage from the U.S. capital—better known by the
sun-kissed daughters and sons of mother Africa as Chocolate City.

Yet, I refuse to believe that my letter will be rejected at heaven's
post office. Why? Because your grace and mercy paid the postage
on this priority letter almost two thousand years ago on the cross
on Calvary. For I am persuaded that Jesus, the Suffering Servant
and Liberator of the oppressed, paid the price on the cross for this
letter to be delivered to you, Almighty God. I also know that "May
I never boast of anything except the cross of our Lord Jesus Christ,
by which the world has been crucified to me, and I to the world,"
to use the language of the apostle Paul (Galatians 6:14). As the
Holy Scriptures further affirm: "And through him God was pleased
to reconcile to himself all things, whether on earth or in heaven, by
making peace through the blood of his cross" (Colossians 1:20).

Almighty God, I do not want to be uninformed concerning either material things or spiritual things. Allow me, therefore, to introduce myself in this letter. I am known as Brotha-man from Washington, D.C. I come from a rich religio-cultural heritage. I attended the Million Man March on October 16, 1995, in our nation's capital. In terms of African heritage, you know, God, that my people were the first to share the cradle of civilization with the world. This was achieved, O God, by my very own people at a time when many of us experienced a climate of persecution and alienation.

From Brotha-man to God, I must confess that once upon a time, I really didn't know much about our own cultural achievements in the universal scheme of things. O God, it seems that so much was hidden from me, growing up black in America. I am puzzled and don't know why so many folks in our multicultural and multiracial society seem to take special license in hiding the truth from me about my history and noble heritage.

O God, it wasn't until recently that I read about your wise servant, Professor Cheikh Anta Diop, who challenged young black brothers like myself to remember that many people of African descent were and are great intellectuals—and not just shoe-shine boys and skycaps at countless international airports throughout our global society. Therefore, "intellectuals ought to study the past," says Diop, "not for the pleasure they find in so doing, but to derive lessons from it." You know, God, I never thought of it that way, but I must admit to the fact that this brother gives to each one of us a lot to ponder. On another occasion, I remember Professor Diop raising the whole critical issue of how the spiritual, moral, and social development of black personality itself has been greatly affected by what he called "a climate of alienation." He rightly declared:

A climate of alienation has a profound effect on the Black personality, particularly on the educated Black, who has the opportunity to see how the rest of the world regards him and his people. It often happens that the Black intellectual thus loses confidence in his own potential and that of his race. Often the effect is so crushing that some Blacks, having evidence to the contrary, still find it hard to accept the fact we really were the first to civilize the world.[1]

Almighty God, I write this letter as a brotha-man because thou art holy, just, and pure. Though the foul odor of racial injustice still lingers, you alone, O God, can cleanse it sure. Like many in my race who attended the Million Man March, I had my doubts, wonders, and concerns whether the organizers of the march would ever reach their goal; but suddenly I realized that in your presence, though we were broken by sin, we would somehow be made whole. I suddenly realized that it wasn't about numbers, but spiritual nurture.

Merciful God, I deeply hunger to know more about black history and the truth and tragedy of my people and their contributions to Western civilization. Some history books deny the reality of our professional achievements in the building of America. When this happens, O God, it makes me feel real bad. It seems to dismantle my own self-confidence.

I get angry so quick, dear God, and feel like giving up. I feel like a doormat: put down and trampled upon. When racial injustices come my way, dear God, I can understand clearly why, for instance, Cheikh Anta Diop, along with other writers and historians, concluded that black men "still find it hard to accept the fact we really were the first to civilize the world." God, this whole business of being the first to civilize the uncivilized is a very heavy matter for my mind to ponder.

Indeed, O God, I think that as I write this letter to heaven's post office, the significance of being the first to civilize is weakened and diminished by the bottomless pit of racism that still engulfs white America. Therefore, it is rather hard, dear God, to motivate and orientate the same people who attended the Million Man March into believing all this stuff about being the first.

In a society where one's very existence is beaten down to the level of second-class citizenship, it takes more than a leap of faith, dear God, to really hold as truth the notion that black people were the first to civilize the world. Existentially, I deeply agonize over this matter. Almighty God, I cry out to thee, not in vexation but in wonderment, as a brotha-man in regard to a reasonable inquiry on who we are.

From Brotha to God, I am compelled to ponder in this perennial climate of alienation the matters of my heritage. O God, how am I to explain to a young black welfare mother that her great African ancestors were the first to civilize the world? How am I to explain this fact of history to black peasants of Brazil who earn less than five hundred dollars a year for their labor? How am I to explain this to a black Mississippi sharecropper who once picked cotton from sun up to sun down? How am I, O God, to explain this to a teenage gang member? How am I to explain this awesome fact of black history to a nineteen-year-old inner-city drug dealer, whose only concern is "Show me the money"? As you might well gather, O God, from the tone of this letter sent overnight express, we as African Americans and other people of color have some serious problems of identity and survival right here on earth!

Almighty God, as a brotha-man, I am both visible and invisible in this wilderness we call white America. It would appear, O Divine Master, that in matters of crime, theft, and violence, the brotha-man is most visible, for better or worse, in the trenches of

American society. But in matters of quality education, strong work ethic, and personal integrity there is the appearance of gross invisibility. Regarding these external perceptions of my being, O God, one is likely to agree with Ralph Ellison's poignantly relevant observation: "I am invisible, understand, simply because people refuse to see me."

Perhaps now it is time to restore faith in the brotha-man. It seems to me, O God, that that is one of the important lessons of the Million Man March. Here the struggle to restore faith in oneself deemed by many to be the most despised and wretched of the earth is not a simple possibility. Rather it is an ethically dangerous point to consider. Can there be no help? Is there no balm in Gilead for the wounded and the wretched? How sublime is justice to injustice? How rugged is the old rugged cross with its emblem of suffering and shame? Loving God, thou art holy and compassionate, but how strong is love for the seemingly unlovable on this planet?

Although I believe and affirm that God's grace is as fathomless as the sea, God's grace stands in the gap between hostility and hospitality, and grace itself is enough for me. Although I believe this to be true and trustworthy, I'm still puzzled, O God, by the fact of our continuing invisibility in American society, especially in traditional seats of white male power and professional respectability.

In the first place, we have a problem down here, O God, with what some folks call affirmative action programs. God, it seems that everywhere I look in this society, I see people in positions of power, authority, and respectability busy at work trying to dismantle affirmative action initiatives. One hears of such moves among a growing number of states through the nation—seemingly bent on turning back the clock to a euphoric period in time that they call the good ol' days.

Well, God, I am indeed a bit puzzled because I can't seem to recall such a Camelot period in time when the landscape of racial and ethnic relations in America reflected a level playing field. O God, I am now straining my brain trying to recall that golden moment in the civil rights movement of the mid-sixties, for instance, when all of a sudden the playing field of opportunity and economic prosperity was magically the same or equal for black and white and for the countless minorities and ethnic groups that seek to obtain a piece of the American dream. I muse internally on this whole problem of affirmative action, O God.

Furthermore, I am inclined to ethically consider the question of whether we have made sufficient racial progress since the turbulent years of the early 1960s that we no longer need such corrective measures as affirmative action now. Has America overcome its racial divide in such a way that we no longer need to worry about the triadic demons of racism, sexism, and classism? Honest to God, if we confess and validate that these vitriolic patterns of sin and greed no longer exist on the American landscape of democracy, then I am willing to concede ethically and politically that the dominant institutions and corporations that run our lives and economy can simply throw all affirmative action programs out the window! But I don't think they can validate that because they know it's a big lie!

O God, it is for this reason, but not this reason only, that I confess to you that Ward Connerly, a leading opponent, was completely off base when he muttered, "We're going to have to start doing away with the silly little boxes that define people by race."

Second, we have a problem down here, Almighty God, with black men abusing black women. The abuse by men of their women and daughters is as staggering as it is morally alarming. Brotha-man, I ask you a simple question, "Who gave you permission to go upside your woman's head whenever you feel like it? Who gave you the green light to use your wife, girlfriend, or lover as a punching bag?" Now if you want, Brotha-man, to get in the ring and box with somebody, why don't you box with God? Why do you beat up on the vulnerable ones in society? Do you want to wrestle or box with angels? Well, be that as it may, there is one thing that stands to reason: Your arms are too short to box with God!

Be not deceived, Brotha-man, I'm not trying to lay a heavy guilt trip on all brothers. But if the shoe fits—wear it! Believe me, Brotha-man, when I say I am not trying to pour out contempt upon your head, or to lay bare the vulnerable strings of black pride, but rather to expose abuse that cannot hide. Brotha-man, I'm trying to suggest that in a world torn by hatred God demands that we render love. Brotha-man, I'm trying to suggest that in a world smashed by ethnic fear, God requires us to render faith. Brotha-man, I'm trying to suggest that in a world deeply burdened by a global economic crisis, render to your sisters, daughters, and all people kindness over cruelty.

Third, Almighty God, we have a problem down here on earth with misplaced aggression in poor and urban communities throughout our society. Of course, from brotha to God, I've been aware of this basic social problem for many moons. It just seems to me, O Divine Master, that in the recent years the problem has escalated to the point where stressed-out people are killing stressed-out people, where teenage mothers are killing their babies at an alarming rate, where sons are killing fathers, and grandsons are assaulting grandmothers.

Fourth, Almighty God, I humbly confess that I, a black man, am guilty of thinking, as a college student, that a white professor with a Ph.D. in natural science knew more than a black professor with a Ph.D. in natural science. So sadly, God, I confess that I favored the white professor over the black professor—maybe I had some silly, naive attitude that, magically, the white man's water was sweeter than the black man's water, that a white physician with the exact same medical training in microbiology as a black one had better skills and knowledge, that a white bank can keep my money—although I have less than two thousand dollars in life's savings—safer than a black bank.

O God, you know that I'm ashamed to admit that I am, indeed, addicted to the main sociopolitical tenets of Anglo-American culture. O God, it would seem that in my quiet moments of reflection on the legacy of the Million Man March, a lesson that no brotha-man dare to forget is one's captivity, seemingly, to white standards of beauty and aesthetics. While skin color should not be a big thing in the United States, there is the nobler view, to paraphrase Dr. King, who once remarked, "A man should not be judged by the color of one's skin but by the content of one's character."

O Gracious God, we all have, undoubtedly, heard this marvelous quotation of Martin Luther King Jr. from time to time. But history, God, seems to be more partial to realism than idealism in our common struggle to make sense out of human experience. If one follows the moral logic of a Derrick Bell or a Cornel West, we are critically reminded that in America, race still matters. The bottom line, O God, is this: I am a recovering intellectual Euroholic. Therefore, from Brotha to God, one needs to pay close attention to the dangers of uncritically aping white culture.

Fifth, Almighty God, the morally honest person must struggle with the fundamental problem of goodness. For example, is the human person—whether black or white—fundamentally good or evil? What ought I to be or do as an individual with some African roots? Why should I be good when others prosper from being bad? To be sure, the perception of brotha-man in the dominant culture may be quite different from the social reality in the lived world of black suffering. Yet I affirm that human beings are born in sin. O God, it seems to me that the gravity of our moral dilemma as humans was perhaps best stated by Paul when he wrote: "For I do not do the good I want, but the evil I do not want is what I do. Now if I do what I do not want, it is no longer I that do it, but sin that dwells in me" (Romans 7:19–20). It has been said and some believe that there is so much good in the worst of us; there is so much bad in the best of us—who can tell the rest of us? The condition of human sin is universal. O God, this moral condition of sinfulness poses a peculiar problem for black men and other folks living in a racist society.

O God, our problem is that we don't always get it right. Even as we struggle with the critical issues of life, we often forget that we are still just sinners saved by your grace (Romans 7:23, 1 Corinthians 15:56, Ephesians 2:8, 2 Corinthians 12:9). As I conclude this letter and my musings to you, O God, how deeply aware I am that we have a moral problem of sin. For example, we often lie, cheat, and steal from one another, so we don't always get it right.

O God, we officially excluded our sisters from the Million Man March, causing pain to many already humiliated by white society's exclusion—we don't always get it right. We have a rate of 50 percent of high school dropouts among inner-city students—we don't always get it right. We have a disproportionate amount of AIDS and crime, reaping a reign of terror on predominantly poor black neighborhoods in urban America. We don't always get it right, O God!

We have black men today still beating and abusing women and children, for no apparent reason under the sun. We don't always get it right!

O God, I deeply agonize over the fact that we have more killings in one year in urban, gang-infested ghettos, of blacks killing other blacks, than lynchings by the Ku Klux Klan in the combined decades of the 1920s, 1930s, and 1940s in American society. We don't always get it right!

O God, as soul brothers who attended the Million Man March and got all fired up after hearing long speeches and inspirational music, I must confess that many of us went back home and did literally nothing to improve the social condition in the neighborhoods in which we live, move, and have our being. We don't always get it right. Therefore, God, as I muse about our situation, our problem morally is not simply one of our blackness and living in a white racist society, but the universal human condition of sin—as ordinary people living on this planet we call earth. But somehow, I can still remember you telling us that God can use simple ordinary people who don't always get it right. But I am so glad that there is a God-force that can help us get it right! Moreover, I'm so glad that trouble won't last always.

And I thank you, God, as your child, as a soul brother, as a brotha-man, that "weeping may endure for a night but joy . . . comes in the morning" (Psalm 30:5). Therefore, I praise you, God, for your goodness and mighty works. As the psalmist declares: "Praise the Lord! O give thanks to the Lord, for he is good; for his steadfast love endures forever. Who can utter the mighty doings of the Lord, or declare all his praise? Happy are those who observe justice, who do righteousness at all times" (Psalm 106:1–3).

Finally, Almighty God, I know that as a brotha-man growing up in America, I also have the strengths and virtues from at least two dominant cultural streams and moral traditions, namely Afrocentrism and Eurocentrism. Therefore, I can rejoice on earth as the angels rejoice in heaven that the creative genius of black personality is a composite image of both cultural and religious traditions. Thus, Joseph said, we can shout from the mountaintop, "They meant it for evil, but God meant it for my good"; and because God was with Joseph, God enabled his circumstance to prosper (Genesis 41:52).

Now, O God, I am beginning to understand more clearly the divine force in this universe, especially in coming to an awareness of responsibility for one's own destiny. As Brother Jesse Jackson said, "No one can save us from us, but us!" On the economic front, Brotha-man, I am gradually scratching the surface of awareness to see that I am not a mere victim of society's misdeeds but a positive actor in history. O God, by this I mean to point out to my sisters and brothers that African Americans, for example, earned $350 billion in annual income in 1996. In 2000 it is estimated that we will earn $900 billion. In America, we spend $225 billion a year on goods and services. Our problem, O God, is not the lack of money, but the lack of cooperative economics and the collective will to trust one another in the efficient use of hard capital to improve the quality of life in communities of color.

O gracious God, I know that it is time for a change in the moral direction of our nation and world.

O gracious God, you are the holy one, whose spirit carved out the rock of African civilization from the mountain of your own being. Open now our eyes that we may see our new identity resting upon thee. Finally, I have never—like all groaning humanity—seen you, O God, but sometimes I can feel you rocking and reshaping the small frame of my world. As I close this letter, I pray that you will continue to rock the small frame of my being until I experience fully your transforming love.

O gracious God, remember the struggles of your people, not for the size of our failures—for they are great—but for the resilience of our spirit to fight for what is right, decent, and equal.

O gracious God, as I close this letter, a letter of utmost concern from Brotha-man, I do so seeking your forgiveness and mercy. There are so many things that I left unsaid in this letter, and there are things I have said that perhaps I should have kept silent. O God, you know them all together. Despite my misdeeds and faults, I hope in this letter, and in the spirit of the Wounded Healer, you will look beyond our faults and see our needs. O God, I fervently pray that you will continue to breathe on the oppressed and downtrodden of every nation and land the spirit that gives us all new life. As always, I eagerly await, in faithfulness, to hear from heaven a word from God.

Sincerely,

Brotha-man

Being Touched by Angels

WHEN HE ENTERED THE HOUSE, THE BLIND MEN CAME TO HIM; AND JESUS SAID TO THEM, "DO YOU BELIEVE THAT I AM ABLE TO DO THIS?" THEY SAID TO HIM, "YES, LORD." THEN HE TOUCHED THEIR EYES AND SAID, "ACCORDING TO YOUR FAITH LET IT BE DONE TO YOU."

—Matthew 9:28–29

THE ANGELS ARE THE DISPENSERS AND ADMINISTRATORS OF THE DIVINE BENEFICENCE TOWARD US; THEY REGARD OUR SAFETY, UNDERTAKE OUR DEFENSE, DIRECT OUR WAYS, AND EXERCISE A CONSTANT SOLICITUDE THAT NO EVIL BEFALL US.

—John Calvin, *Institutes of the Christian Religion*

The diverse crowds of people that constituted that special event called the Million Man March shared one organic gift, despite differences in ideology, religion, class, or sexual or lifestyle orientation—the will to believe. For ordinary people of struggle, the will to believe is the power of being. The will to believe is power to see the unseen. The will to believe is the power to reach the unreachable. The will to believe is the power to touch the untouchable.

In retrospect, there were loads of American citizens, black and white, who had a deep suspicion and skepticism that the march would even take place. From an ideological point of view, many God-fearing folk had difficulty with Minister Louis Farrakhan's perceived philosophy of radical black nationalism and separatism. Some skeptics argued that the proposed march was untimely and immaterial because it seemed to some, strategically speaking, to alienate and strain patterns of traditional black leadership among the major civil rights organizations—especially those, for instance, like the NAACP and National Urban League, which depended in the mid-sixties on white financial support from corporate America.

Other skeptics believed that the whole idea of the march was ill advised and divisive because it formally excluded women, over half of the U.S. population. The will to believe did not dampen the spirit, apparently, of those who got on the bus and made the pilgrimage to Washington, D.C.—Chocolate City—or those who elected by ideology and conscience to simply stay at home.

The Will to Believe

The will to believe is a persistent virtue among all ethnic groups, classes, colors, nationalities, and religions that make up the universal tapestry of the human family. But for people of African descent, the will to believe is a peculiar sensation emanating from a profound integration of religion and culture: a sort of internal feeling inherent in the very soul of black personalities that there is no separation between the sacred and the profane.

The Cartesian dualism so pervasive in Anglo-Western thought—which tends to sharply compartmentalize mind and body, head and heart, the material and spiritual realms—has no place of dominance in the African worldview. For Africans, religion affirms life, and life affirms religion. Africans live in a spiritual universe. So then, the will to believe as the power to reach the unreachables was part of the spirit behind the Million Man March. To be sure, the will to believe as the power to touch the untouchables was a deep moral theme behind the Million Man March, or so it seems to me.

Within the conflicted rhythms of my own soul, I believe and affirm that to be touched by angels means to be touched by God, the creator and the merciful one. To be touched by angels means to be guided, energized, and healed by the radical love of God as revealed in Jesus Christ. To be touched by angels means not placing too much stock in the armchair critic who must leave his armchair if he is to uncover truth and find new life. To be touched by angels means that the perennial search for truth may take us down roads less traveled. *To be touched by angels* means a gradual awareness that the faithful sojourner who responds to truth has always been a minority rather than a large crowd of people. In short, to be touched by angels means an openness on the part of the believer to the healing of one's wounded spirit—not by grit, but by God's grace.

I believed then, as I believe now, that some of us need the healing touch of the Master's hand. In this sense, the Million Man March was an invitation to a sort of communal cleansing of the heart, mind, body, and soul. Metaphorically, it is as if Jesus would directly ask the contemporary people of society, "Do you believe that I am able to do this?" They would say to him, "Yes, Lord." Then he would touch their eyes and say, "According to your faith let it be done to you" (Matthew 9:28–29). Is this not one of the significant moral lessons behind the Million Man March? Can we really afford the absence of a basic belief system in a world of pain and racial oppression? Can we afford the absence of belief in the power of one's being to be touched by angels? Could it be that many of us have already been guided or touched by angels and are unaware?

Why Not Remember Airport Angels?

I recall my early morning trip from Lambert International Airport in St. Louis, Missouri, on the morning of the Million Man March, during a quiet autumn day as trees proudly displayed a mosaic of bright red, gold, and yellow leaves of the season. The image of airport angels refers to real black sisters who loved their black brothers—and the cause for which we journeyed—enough to get out of bed in the wee hours of the dawn to serve as airport hosts.

I took this challenging trip seriously, arriving at the airport at 4:00 A.M. en route to Washington, D.C. Like a pilgrimage to Mecca, I felt compelled to journey to Washington, as one solitary voice amidst a colossal floodgate of humanity that came from every corner of the nation: from Birmingham to Boston, from New York to New Mexico.

I vividly remember on the early morning of October 16 the beaming and bright faces of young black women, dressed in white—apparently from a local branch of the Nation of Islam— who served as flight greeters, guardians, and guardian angels to guide us more efficiently through the security points in the airport. Historically, it is significant to observe that never before in the cultural narrative of this country have so many African American men peacefully gathered to pray, sing, reflect, and celebrate a sense of oneness and spiritual solidarity. While there, we wandered about the Washington Mall observing and listening to the ideas, lyrics, and theological chants of poets, preachers, and politicians—all seemingly having a different point of view, but ironically pointing toward a common good, despite the ideological divisions highlighted by the critics and skeptics in the mass media.

What Did the Bible Say?

The provocative question "What did the Bible say?" is one that puzzles the critical mind and teases the prophetic imagination of the believer. It is not a question for the hard-nosed skeptic, who may doubt the very existence of God as the ground and source of our being, as the creator and maker of heaven and earth. But for the believer or supporter of the Million Man March, the question itself is sweet music to one's spiritual ear. For we have been told by the African elders and wise ones of old that faith comes by "hearing, and hearing by the Living Word of God" (Romans 10:17). Therefore, I submit to you that the Bible is clear about the reality and guiding presence of angels.

Biblically considered, an angel (Hebrew *malák,* Greek *angelos*) is, etymologically and theologically, a messenger of God.[1] An angel is a being higher than humankind, certainly a creature, but also a heavenly being—uncorrupted in its original essence—who possesses free will and has the authority to resist sin and evil in the world. Parenthetically, the Bible even speaks of angels who sin. Indeed, Satan is a fallen angel: "God did not spare the angels who sinned" says the Bible, "but consigned them to the dark pits of hell, where they are reserved for judgment" (2 Peter 2:4, Revelation 12:9, Matthew 25:41). In a deeply human sense, angels are often depicted as mortal messengers of the Divine who try to get our attention as children of God in need of a new revelation. Accordingly, Alexander Whyte in *The Nature of Angels* boldly observed regarding the role of angels in Hebraic history: "God took the form, and came in the character, of an angel when he conveyed anything new or confirmed any old revelation of grace or truth to the Hebrew people."[2]

The drama of Hebraic history always involved angels or Yahweh's special messengers of hope and deliverance in times of suffering and brokenness. Indeed, the wilderness experience of the ancient Hebrew people serves as a vital moral link in our understanding of the contemporary experiences of suffering and oppression on the part of African Americans and other people of color. Just as God took the form or character of angels on behalf of the liberation and well-being of ancient Hebrews, this same God of the Bible can do anything but fail in the interest of blacks and the marginalized people in our global community today. To be sure, there are guardian angels camped out around us, working on behalf of God's realm of love and righteousness in oppressed communities throughout the world—if only one could see through faith's eye. And any of us can be instruments of God:

I Believe

I believe as night gives way
To break of day,
Love is the only power that will stay.
I believe as others seek advantage
Through insidious gain,
Love's mighty power enables
Us to endure the pain.

I believe every golden leaf
Which falls from the tree,
Somehow replenishes the earth
And blesses me.
I believe there is sunlight
Behind every darkened day,
Groping beneath shadows
To show us the way.

So, Lord Jesus, help me to so live
And to believe in Thee,
That those who know me and know
Thee not will want to know more about Thee,
Because they know me.[3]

For some people, the mere contemplation of the notion of angels is a profoundly disturbing thing, because it tends to put the modern liberal Christian or rationalist out of control. As humans, we just love to think that we are in control of the universe, of the world's systems of knowledge and power. Philosophically, we have been bitten by the Promethean bugs of self-sufficiency and possessive individualism that quietly echo the collective consciousness of modern culture: "Man is the measure of all things," "Look out for number one," or "Grab for all the gusto" because you only go around once in life. Sayings like these saturate and penetrate our consumer culture, like the latest advertising gimmicks from Wall Street. They tend to dull our ethical sensibility to mystery and the importance of solitude. They negate our affection for the Divine. And they tend to obscure, rationally, one's contemplation of a belief system inclusive of angels.

From an African American religio-historical perspective, however, the good news is that "we have been believers believing in the black gods of an old land." Perhaps this observation of the will to believe is tied in deeply with what it means to be black living in America now. Existentially speaking, I suspect that if we were to take a leaf from the notebook of angels, their message to us would be: "Remember, you are never alone; I am with you in the wilderness of your pain and suffering, despite injustices, and the profound contradictions of life." Compare the angelic appearances to Hagar in the wilderness (Genesis 16:7–13, 21:17–20), to Abraham on Mt. Moriah (Genesis 22:11–18), and to Moses in the burning bush (Exodus 3:2). Scripture also testifies to the fact that angels are spiritual beings separate from God, but of deep integrity, goodwill, and obedience to the Divine (cf. 1 Samuel 29:9, 2 Samuel 14:17, 20, Judges 6:11–23, 1 Kings 19:5–7).

To illustrate the nature and role of angels in human history, the esteemed evangelist Billy Graham, in his book entitled *Angels,* wrote:

> Angels are God's secret agents. . . . As God's angels have watched the drama of this age unfolding they have seen the Christian church established and expand around the world. They miss nothing as they watch the movement of time, "to the intent . . . that the principalities and powers in heavenly places might be known by the Church, the manifold wisdom of God" (Ephesians 3:10).[4]

Now for the Christian community of faith, I think that it is critically important to remember how angels played a special role in the redemptive and transformative elements of the resurrection story. For instance, David Jeremiah's recent book *What the Bible Says about Angels* describes passionately the pivotal role of angels in the resurrection narrative:

> The night is over. Dawn is here. . . . We see soldiers, tired from a long . . . night, standing guard at a hillside Tomb. . . . Suddenly, the ground is shaking. An angel appears out of nowhere, coming as fast as a lightning bolt and just as bright. . . . The angel moves a massive stone that covers the mouth of the Tomb. He rolls it aside effortlessly, then calmly sits down on top of it.[5]

For the human community, the bottom line is that angels are messengers of God who help finite creatures like us in times of danger, mortal need, cultural disorientation, family disintegration, and the crisis of faith that causes us to wonder whether we will ever overcome the burden of racism in white America. Could angels be our hidden protectors like in the movie *The Preacher's Wife?* Could angels be our invisible bodyguards? Could angels possibly be our secret weapon against white racism in America?

Well, brothers and sisters, the good news is that while racism may be a permanent feature of American culture, according to Derrick Bell, in his critically acclaimed book *Faces at the Bottom of the Well,* people are not born racist.[6] Babies are born babies. People are born people. People from whatever culture or religious persuasion acquire the habits of both race and religion after birth, not before.

Put another way, cultural habits of the heart that reflect racism, for example, can be changed by divine habits of love that reflect the healing presence of God under the guidance of angels. Let me now share a true story with you concerning the healing presence and guidance of angels.

Angels and a Time of Reckoning

It was a cool, clear Sunday morning in September 1993. At 10:00 A.M. the pattern of traffic was unusually heavy as I made my way from Limuru to the Jomo Kenyetta International Airport in Nairobi, Kenya. I was on the first leg of a circular travel research seminar, with a final destination along the mountainous borders between Zimbabwe and South Africa. I first had to journey by plane over a perilous terrain known among pilots as the "zone of rocky turbulence"!

Well, by the time I arrived at the airport in the city of Harare, I was sick as a dog. Rev. Dr. Fred Gomez, former president of United Theological College and my host, was there to meet me— right on time. After a brief traditional African greeting, "Jambo," my colleague Fred sensed the pain of my personal discomfort and drove me immediately to the home of his personal physician to receive proper medical care for my illness.

Fred's personal physician, a graduate of one of the best medical schools in London, diagnosed my case as acute nausea and dizziness and thereby prescribed the appropriate medicine, which I took faithfully for three days. But there was a basic problem: the prescription given did not correct or remedy my upset stomach or ease the perennial dizziness that I suffered. Based on my previously scheduled travel seminar, I had two major lectures to give at United Theological College on the fourth day of my campus visit, and I was near the end of my rope. A day of reckoning was about to appear, and I was still not well.

And then I began to reason and agonize deep within myself, "Is there no balm in Gilead? Is there no physician or guardian angel there?" To my surprise, my story of personal affliction had, apparently, made the local *New York Times* on campus, and almost out of nowhere a seminary student who was regarded by peers as a healer in the customary traditions of African culture and religion appeared. As a North American Christian and political liberal, I was exceedingly suspicious and skeptical of what might be called spiritual healing. But on the eve of my third day of illness, I reluctantly gave it a try—though I still find it hard and somewhat embarrassing to talk about.

The precise time of reckoning and the testing of my own faith came at 9:00 A.M. on the fourth day of my campus visit at United, as the student healer and I entered the Divine Mercy Chapel. He quietly and almost silently instructed me to pray along with him, while placing my hand on that part of the body racked by pain. I did as the spiritual healer instructed. The actual prayer time, I must confess, was not long. It was less than one minute.

I don't know the secrets of African healing or prayer life. Rationally, I do know that it was not magic or a psychic form of witchcraft, lost in the art of African rituals and tribal ceremonies.

What I am certain about is simply this: as I left the chapel, my pain was gone; my illness had ceased, dried up like a raisin in the sun. Later in the week, I suddenly discovered, while living on campus, that this student healer came from a family in the rural areas of Zimbabwe. His father was a spiritualist and healer who believed in the healing power of angels.

I was struck by his ethical sensitivity and the force of his African spirituality. As I learned later, this young seminarian grew up in the district of Chipinge, which is located in the Manica Province in the republic of Zimbabwe. Now in this traditional village community of seven hundred people, there is a popular African proverb that goes: "When I dance with angels, the face of sickness banishes." Around the flourishing fields of village life—where maize, peas, and beans are seasonally harvested—there is plenty of good room for dancing and singing the joyful melodies of the gospel of Jesus Christ. Mothers and daughters dance and sing about the redeeming power of God. Fathers and sons join in the communal religious chorus, as showers of praise go up to the living God for blessings and healings, and as angels gaze on in wonderment and adoration to the Supreme Creator of heaven and earth.

Angels are the powerful messengers of God who can do God's bidding in times of sickness and adversity in human society. They are ministering spirits sent by God to accomplish a divine purpose and to bless the hurting ones victimized by the injustices and contradictions of history. Therefore, angels are moral mediators who obediently do the bidding of Almighty God. Hence, the psalmist declares: "Bless the Lord, O you his angels, you mighty ones who do his bidding, obedient to his spoken word. Bless the Lord, all his hosts, his ministers that do his will. Bless the Lord, all his works, in all places of his dominion. Bless the Lord, O my soul" (Psalm 103:20–22).

As an African American Christian and theologian, I affirm and believe that angels do, in fact, exist, although rationally I have not been at this place for long in my own critical thinking. Perhaps it was my Augustinian pride or the bankrupt liberal theology of nineteenth-century Enlightenment thought that played tricks on my critical moral judgment. Perhaps it was the conflicted dialectic of what Reinhold Niebuhr calls the perennial tensions between realism and idealism in modern Christian thought that negated, existentially, my appreciation for the role of angels in human affairs. Perhaps it was my preoccupation with Dr. King's brilliant articulation of the ethical problematic for blacks, namely, the problem of powerless morality versus immoral power, that prevented me from understanding more clearly the role of angels in the biblical materials. I don't really know the exact source for this inward ambivalence and uneasiness about angels.

But I do know and believe, as attested by Holy Scriptures, that angels are real beings. Angels are the special agents of God's divine mercy and grace. I affirm and believe that angels can appear or disappear at the command of God. For people with a shared memory of suffering and oppression, angels are God-sent messengers of liberation and healing. In this sense, angels mediate the justice and mercy of God in a world that seems to show neither justice nor mercy toward the poor and marginalized peoples on the planet earth. Yet through the mystery of God's love and grace, angels are the mighty ones who do God's bidding, obedient to God's spoken word.

As for the legacy of the Million Man March, I affirm and believe that God's liberating activity and healing grace were present among people I met and heard. To be sure, I believe the guardian angels of life undoubtedly hovered over that big crowd that no man or statistics expert could number; perhaps the angels flew so high as to be beyond our human sight, but they were always looking down upon us.

In short, I affirm and believe that many of us who attended the Million Man March perhaps went there unaware that we were not alone. We had a company of angels—seen and unseen—who rode the buses and vans, boarded the airplanes, and rode shotgun as the invisible seventh passenger in countless automobiles that streamed across the interstate highways of America en route to the nation's capital on that day.

What is important about angels in light of the legacy of the Million Man March? What is worth remembering as African American sojourners living in a strange land? Well, I can't speak for others, but as for me and my own faith pilgrimage to the Washington Mall, the angels are those benevolent beings who continue to journey with us through our wilderness experiences.

Ethically and religiously considered, angels are the silver linings amid the clouds. Angels are peacemakers in the midst of family feuds and the social disintegration of the black community. Angels are symbolic of the stabilizing anchors in the midst of the stormy seas of life. Certainly if the biblical truth is told, I suspect that angels function as the midnight wrestlers who struggle hard to bless us in spite of our wrongdoing and sin before the crack of dawn, as one did for the biblical Jacob. For my own ragtag faith, angels are as real as the air we breathe, and as solid as the rock of our salvation, despite the shifting sands of politics and religion so pervasive on the contemporary American scene.

Now as I left the Washington Mall to return to St. Louis on that special evening of October 16, the lingering question upon my lips that still echoes in my heart was, "Have you ever been touched by an angel?"

Notes

Open Letter to the Man on the Mall

1. J. D. Douglas, ed., *The New Bible Dictionary,* Grand Rapids, Mich.: Eerdman's Publishing Co., 1973), 107. See also Donald MacPherson Baillie, *God Was in Christ;* J. Denney, *The Christian Doctrine of Reconciliation;* Vincent Taylor, *The Atonement in New Testament Teaching;* and Karl Barth, *Church Dogmatics,* vol. 4 (New York: Charles Scribner's Sons, 1956).

2. Francis Brown, ed., *The New Hebrew and English Lexicon* (Peabody, Mass.: Hendrickson Publishers, 1979), 497.

3. Douglas, *New Bible Dictionary,* 107–8.

4. Ibid., 107–9.

5. *Emerge: Black America's New Magazine,* February 1996, 56.

6. Cited in Andrew Hacker, *Two Nations: Black and White, Separate, Hostile, Unequal* (New York: Ballantine Books, 1992), 243ff.

7. Vincent Harding, *There Is a River* (New York: Harcourt Brace Jovanovich, 1981), xii.

8. Ibid., 3–26ff.

9. See Robert M. Franklin, *Liberating Visions* (Minneapolis: Fortress Press, 1990), 20ff.

10. See "The Most Influential People In America, 1997," *Time,* April 21, 1997.

Ten Principles of Black Self-Esteem

1. Gene H. Outka and Paul Ramsey, eds., *Norm and Context in Christian Ethics* (New York: Charles Scribner's Sons, 1968), 3–4ff.

2. Jay David, ed., *Growing Up Black* (New York: Avon Books, 1992), 36–41ff.

3. *Ebony,* November 1957.

4. See Cliff Farmer, "Seminary Address: Faith and Philosophy," lecture at Eden Seminary Chapel, St. Louis, 1991.

5. John S. Mbiti, *African Religions and Philosophies* (New York: Anchor Books, 1970), 76.

6. Malcolm X, in *Famous Black Quotations,* ed. Janet Cheatham Bell (Chicago: Sabart Publications, 1986), 43.

7. E. Hammond Oglesby, *Plumbline: Poems That Heal the Wounded Spirit* (St. Louis: Creative J's Publishers, 1990), 35–36ff.

8. Cheikh Anta Diop, in *Famous Black Quotations,* 28.

9. Cheikh Anta Diop, *The African Origin of Civilization: Myth or Reality* (Westport, Conn.: Lawrence Hill & Co., 1974), xiv.

10. Ibid., 262ff.

11. Benjamin Quarles, *The Negro in the Making of America* (New York: Macmillan, 1969), 22.

12. Winthrop D. Jordan, *White over Black: American Attitudes toward the Negro, 1550–1812* (Baltimore: Penguin Books, 1969), 24ff.

13. Quarles, *The Negro in the Making of America,* 33ff.

14. Ibid., 22.

15. Martin Luther King Jr., *I Have a Dream: The Quotations of Martin Luther King Jr.,* ed. Lotte Hoskins (New York: Grosset and Dunlap Publishers, 1968), 104.

16. O'Neal Shyne Jr., "Preaching to Build Self-Esteem in the Local Church Setting," D.Min. thesis, United Theological Seminary, Dayton, Ohio, 1991, 13–15ff.

17. Roger G. Betsworth, *Social Ethics: An Examination of American Moral Traditions* (Louisville: Westminster John Knox Press, 1990), 53.

18. Ibid., 54.

19. Dietrich Bonhoeffer, *The Cost of Discipleship* (London: SCM Press, 1959).

20. Charles Dickens, cited in *The New Dictionary of Thought: A*

Cyclopedia of Quotations, ed. Tryon Edwards (New York: Standard Book Co., 1964) 84.

21. King, *"I Have a Dream,"* 74ff.

Open Letter from Father to Son

1. Kenneth B. Clark, *Dark Ghetto: Dilemmas of Social Power* (New York: Harper & Row, 1965).

2. Enoch H. Oglesby, "Reachable Dreams," in *Collaboration: A Collection of Poems* (St. Louis: Rycraw Productions, 1991), 79.

Making Small and Large Differences

1. Marian Wright Edelman, in *Black Pearls: Daily Meditations, Affirmations, and Inspirations for African Americans,* ed. Eric V. Copage (New York: Quill William Morrow & Co., 1993).

2. Robert Swenson, *The Ambassador: Promise Keepers* (Boulder, Colo.: Ambassador Ministries, 1990), 6.

3. Ibid.

4. Ibid.

5. Ibid.

6. Ibid.

7. Bill Bright et al., *Seven Principles of a Promise Keeper* (Colorado Springs: Promise Keepers, 1994), 8–9ff.

8. E. Hammond Oglesby, "Conflicting Methodologies in Ethics," lecture at Eden Theological Seminary, St. Louis, October 1997.

9. Theodore Walker Jr., *Empower the People: Social Ethics for the African-American Church* (Maryknoll, N.Y.: Orbis Books, 1991), 91–94. Among ethical sources for guidance in the social context, Walker provides the reader with a cogently relevant analysis of Marian Wright Edelman's "An Agenda for Empowerment," which has to do with the critical issue of accountability for the empowerment of black children and the strengthening of black families, a dominant theme of the Million Man March. Also see Paul Lehmann's clas-

sic work in the methodology of contextualism entitled *Ethics in a Christian Context* (New York: Harper & Row, 1963), 45–73.

10. See James H. Cone, *For My People: Black Theology and the Black Church* (Maryknoll, N.Y.: Orbis Books, 1984), 54–74, and Lehmann, *Ethics in a Christian Context.*

11. Robert Swenson, *The Point Man: Promise Keepers* (Boulder, Colo.: Point Man Ministries, 1990), 2.

12. Ibid., 5.

13. Louis Farrakhan, keynote address, public event in St. Louis, October 4, 1997. After his address, Minister Farrakhan was given a proclamation from Council Freeman Bosley Sr., the father of former St. Louis mayor Freeman Bosley Jr. We may note that the proclamation was in honor of Minister Farrakhan's service to the black community and was a focal point spiritually in preparation for the second anniversary of the Million Man March/Holy Day of Atonement on October 16, 1997.

14. Ibid.

15. "Gateway Arch Rally Resources," handouts at second anniversary of the Million Man March, St. Louis, October 16, 1997.

16. Ibid.

17. Nibs Stroupe and Inez Fleming, *While We Run This Race: Confronting the Power of Racism in a Southern Church* (Maryknoll, N.Y.: Orbis Books, 1995), 14.

18. Ibid., 15–21.

19. Andrew Hacker, *Two Nations: Black and White, Separate, Hostile, Unequal* (New York: Charles Scribner's Sons, 1992), 3.

20. See "Editorial on Race," *The Riverfront Times* (St. Louis), November 5–11, 1997.

21. W. E. B. DuBois, *The Souls of Black Folk* (New York: Fawcett Publications, 1961), 16–17.

22. C. Eric Lincoln, *Coming through the Fire: Surviving Race and Peace in America* (Durham, N.C.: Duke University Press, 1996), 45–46.

23. James Weldon Johnson, in Barry N. Schwartz and Robert Disch, *White Racism: Its History, Pathology, and Practice* (New York: Dell Publishing Co., 1970), 1–2.

24. Louis B. Weeks, *Making Ethical Decision: A Casebook* (Philadelphia: Westminster, 1987), 25ff.

25. Enoch H. Oglesby et al., *Collaboration: A Collection of Poems* (St. Louis: Rycraw Productions, 1991), 70.

Open Letter from Father to Daughter

1. Phillis Wheatley, "On Being Brought from Africa to America," in *Black American Literature,* ed. Ruth Miller (Beverly Hills: Glencoe Press, 1971), 34.

2. Ibid., 35.

Lifting Up an Afrocentric Biblical Legacy

1. Randall C. Bailey and Jacquelyn Grant, eds., *The Recovery of Black Presence: An Interdisciplinary Exploration* (Nashville: Abingdon Press, 1995), 7.

2. Ibid., 8. See also Charles B. Copher, *Black Biblical Studies: An Anthology of Charles B. Copher* (Chicago: Blacklight Fellowship, 1993).

3. Bailey and Grant, *The Recovery of Black Presence,* 8.

4. William Mosley, *What Color Was Jesus?* (Chicago: African American Images, 1987), vii.

5. James H. Evans Jr., *We Have Been Believers* (Minneapolis: Fortress Press, 1992), 77–83ff.

6. Enoch H. Oglesby, *Clues from God's Divine Arithmetic* (Nashville: Townsend Press, 1985), 108ff.

7. Evans, *We Have Been Believers,* 152ff.

Open Letter from Brotha to Brotha

1. DuBois, *The Souls of Black Folk,* 16–17.

Recovering Hope from Martin and Malcolm

1. Malcolm X and Alex Haley, *The Autobiography of Malcolm X* (New York: Grone Press, 1964), 54ff.

2. Stephen B. Oates, *Let the Trumpet Sound* (New York: Harper & Row, 1982).

3. Preston N. Williams, "The Ethics of Black Power," in *Quest for a Black Theology,* ed. J. J. Gardiner and J. Deotis Roberts (Philadelphia: United Church Press, 1971), 82–83ff.

4. Peter I. Rose, *They and We: Racial and Ethnic Relations in the United States* (New York: McGraw-Hill, 1997), 254.

5. Malcolm X, *Malcolm X Speaks: Selected Speeches and Statements,* ed. George Breitman (New York: Grove Weidenfeld, 1965), 99ff.

6. Marcus Garvey, in *Famous Black Quotations,* 60.

7. Malcolm X and Haley, *The Autobiography of Malcolm X,* 6–10ff.

8. Malcolm X, *Malcolm X Speaks,* 210.

9. Martin Luther King Jr., *The Trumpet of Conscience* (New York: Harper & Row, 1967), 69.

10. Martin Luther King Jr., *Stride toward Freedom* (New York: Harper & Row, 1958), 21ff.

11. James H. Cone, *Martin, Malcolm, and America: A Dream or a Nightmare?* (Maryknoll, N.Y.: Orbis Books, 1991), 290–93ff.

12. Martin Luther King Jr., *Where Do We Go from Here: Chaos or Community?* (Boston: Beacon Press, 1967), 190–93ff.

13. C. Eric Lincoln and Lawrence H. Mamiya, *The Black Church in the African American Experience* (Durham, N.C.: Duke University Press, 1990), 10.

14. Ibid., 11.

15. Ibid., 9–10.

16. Ibid., 12–15ff.

17. Cited in Cone, *Martin, Malcolm, and America,* 252.

18. Oglesby, "Did You Get the Point," in *Collaboration,* 71.

19. Johnson, cited in Schwartz and Disch, *White Racism,* 1–2.

20. Enoch H. Oglesby, *Living at the Intersection of Race and Religion* (St. Louis: Eden Seminary Publication, 1995), 17.

Open Letter from Brotha to Sister

1. Alice Walker, in *Famous Black Quotations,* 10.

2. See, for example, Constance Willard Williams, *Black Teenage Mothers: Pregnancy and Child Rearing from Their Perspective* (Toronto: Lexington Books, 1991), 8–16.

3. DeLois C. Nance, *Urban Realities* (Chicago, 1990), 26.

Telling the Stories of Black Culture

1. Gregory Baum, "Peter Berger's Unfinished Symphony," in *Sociology and Human Destiny,* ed. Gregory Baum (New York: The Seabury Press, 1980), 112ff.

2. By mythopoetic I mean a moral perspective that combines elements of myth and story as a way to enhance self-esteem and to derive meaning from human experience.

3. Charles E. Morton, *The Ideological Character of Moral Judgment* (St. Louis: Hodale Press, 1996), 5.

4. Ibid., 7.

5. Oglesby, *Clues from God's Divine Arithmetic,* 73ff.

Open Letter from Brotha to God

1. Diop, in *Famous Black Quotations,* 28.

2. Martin Luther King Jr., *The Trumpet of Conscience* (New York: Harper & Row, 1967), 77.

Being Touched by Angels

1. Douglas, *The New Bible Dictionary,* 37ff.

2. Alexander Whyte, *The Nature of Angels* (Grand Rapids: Baker Books, 1995), 95–100ff.

3. Oglesby, "I Believe," in *Collaboration*, 78.

4. Billy Graham, *Angels* (London: Word Publishing, 1994), 176.

5. David Jeremiah, *What the Bible Says about Angels* (Sisters, Ore.: Questar Publishers, 1996), 220–21ff.

6. Derrick Bell, *Faces at the Bottom of the Well* (New York: Basic Books, 1992).